GARDENERS' WORLD

GROW SOMETHING
DIFFERENT

D0271163

To my family who encouraged me to grow plants
from an early age; my girlfriend, Lisa, whose patience
I have much appreciated during the writing of this book
(and who despite all this is still planning to marry me),
and to the late Dr Mark Smith, who shared with me
his enthusiasm and gave me the opportunity to
grow a wide range of plants as a student.

GROW SOMETHING
DIFFERENT

NICK WRAY

BCA

LONDON   NEW YORK   SYDNEY   TORONTO

ACKNOWLEDGEMENTS

I would like to acknowledge the help of the staff at the University Botanic Garden, Bristol for their hard work with many of the plantings and their co-operation during photography; Cannington College, Cannington, Somerset for their use of many of their superb mature plantings in their grounds and Anthony de Grey Trellises, London. My thanks also to Nicky Copeland, my commissioning editor, for her faith in my idea of microclimates and her work in helping me plan this book; Vanessa Daubney, my editor, to whom I am indebted for her guidance and hard work in the completion of this book; Christopher Drew, photographer, for his time and patience in taking many of the beautiful photographs and for his frequent visits to the botanic garden, often at short notice, and Judith Robertson for her work on the design of this book.

This edition published 1995
by BCA
by arrangement with BBC Books,
an imprint of BBC Worldwide Publishing,
BBC Worldwide Ltd, Woodlands,
80 Wood Lane, London W12 0TT

First published 1995
© Nicholas Wray 1995
The moral right of the author has been asserted

CN 1248

Illustrations by Jane Leyster Paige and Will Giles
Designed by Judith Robertson

Set in Bembo
Printed and bound in Great Britain by Butler &
Tanner Limited, Frome and London
Colour separation by Radstock Reproductions
Limited, Midsomer Norton
Cover printed by Richard Clays Limited, Bungay

Front cover:
Callistemon pallidus *(see page 55) and*
Cordyline australis *(see page 53).*

Back cover:
Meconopsis *x* sheldonii *(see page 121).*

Page 1:
Campsis radicans *(see page 61).*

Page 5:
Lysichiton americanus *(see page 83).*

Contents

~

Introduction

∽

I've always been interested in growing many different types of plants, first as a child at home and then in my first job after leaving school. But my eyes were really opened up to the immense variety of the plant world when I went to work at the University of Bristol Botanic Garden as a student. It was from this point that I began to understand that the correct positioning of a plant is very important. All around me were the exotic and the unusual and I wanted to know how to grow them. Why was it that one plant up against a sheltered wall would thrive and another of the same species a short distance away die?

I learnt by my mistakes and these hard lessons led me to become more interested in local variations of climate – the garden's microclimates. Any gardener can identify areas of their garden that have a different feel – a sunny corner, a sheltered wall or a shaded border – and once this has been done growing strong healthy plants can become much easier, as I discovered.

Inspired by earlier successes, I decided to replant a long border with plants grouped into three distinctive zones – woodland, temperate and Mediterranean. The careful positioning and planting of these three zones was televized for *Gardeners' World* and formed part of a mini series on microclimates in the garden. It was as a result of this that I decided to write *Grow Something Different* to explain how you can examine your own garden, paying attention to its microclimates as well as its general location and other features, such as the soil and the garden's vulnerability to winds. All these things are discussed in the first chapter, 'Discovering Your Garden's Potential'. In addition I have included some advice on how to deal with common problems, such as improving your soil. Few of us have the perfect soil in our gardens. If you are lucky it might be all right for growing a fairly decent range of plants, but often it is unsuitable for the ones you are particularly interested in. Therefore it is more than likely that it will need improving in some way.

Following this chapter are six more containing profiles of over fifty plants together with suggestions of numerous varieties other than the ones featured which you might like to try growing. These six chapters fall roughly into two groups: those which appreciate warm, sunny conditions and those which prefer moist, shady positions.

Each main profiled plant is illustrated, but in every entry you'll find a description of it with important background information on its origins and growing preferences, plus how large it is likely to grow and what temperature it will tolerate. In addition there are four other sections which deal with the plant's cultivation (the best location, the type of soil it needs and how to plant it); its requirements for feeding, pruning and winter protection and whether or not it is susceptible to any pests or diseases; how to propagate the plant and, finally, my recommendations for other varieties of the species which I think are worth trying too. I have also suggested which other plants will look good with it. Often these are featured in the same chapter or section, but occasionally I have recommended other quite common plants which are just as easy to grow and with which you may already be familiar.

At the end of each chapter there is a group of mini plant profiles. Selecting the plants that are featured in this book was hard and these plants could easily have been given full entries had there been room. Every one has essential details, such as height and spread (H & S) and temperature tolerance, and a brief physical description. Once you have read the respective chapter, it will be easy to understand the general conditions that these plants prefer and you should have few problems in growing them.

I have grown all the plants featured in this book at one time or another and it never ceases to amaze me how much more attractive a garden looks when one or more of them are growing in it. The blaze of colour presented by some of the tender and hardy sun-loving plants brightens any aspect, while the striking foliage of some of the desert plants accentuates many a border and the lush, but often delicate and elegant, foliage of the moisture-loving and shade-loving plants gives focus to areas that have been overlooked in the past.

My hope is that armed with this book, gardeners can begin to select the special plants that will thrive in the conditions offered by the microclimates in their gardens. With thorough soil preparation, careful siting and planting and some simple winter protection, many beautiful and unusual plans which were previously thought of as difficult to cultivate can now be grown to perfection.

N. J. um

Discovering Your Garden's Potential

~

No matter where you live, nor what aspect it faces, your garden will almost certainly contain some small area that has a climate all of its own: it could be a sun trap with lots of light and warmth, a frost pocket that is slow to thaw out, a sunny south wall, a shady border under some existing trees, or a side passageway where the wind funnels down. Every gardener can identify with at least one of these areas and some they may want to be rid of, like the frost pocket. These climatic deviations from the general conditions in your garden are called microclimates, and whilst microclimates may comprise just a small part of your garden, they can also cover all of it, depending on the garden's situation in relation to the area in which it is located. With a knowledge of the microclimate conditions in your garden and how they affect the plants you can grow, the degree of success you can have with plants may be greatly increased.

Information on individual plants abounds and, with an ever increasing range of gardening books, magazines and television programmes available, some might say it is confusing. But these sources are invaluable in providing lots of background details about the more unusual plants that are becoming popular. Some of this information can be found on the plant label at the nursery or garden centre, but often a little reading will reveal that the plant you want to grow requires some special conditions in order for it to flourish or indeed survive at all, so it's well worth jotting down a few notes about its needs. For example, you should consider the minimum temperature that the plant

~

South-facing walls provide the perfect environment for sun-loving shrubs such as the beautiful yellow-flowered Fremontodendron californicum *(page 58) which grows well with* Abutilon x suntense.

9

can stand, the amount of light it needs, its tolerance of strong winds, soil preference, including the alkalinity or acidity requirements, the amount of water it likes and whether or not the plant will require winter protection in your area.

EXAMINING YOUR MICROCLIMATES

When dealing with slightly more demanding garden plants, it is always best to think first of what they require in order to grow well, rather than where you would like to see them in the garden. You must give the plants what they need or else face disappointment. Once you have discovered if a plant requires special conditions, you must decide where in the garden you can provide, or attempt to provide, those conditions.

Finding out more about your garden and its location is vital in order to build up an accurate picture of the variety of growing conditions. Many of these facts will be to hand, especially if you have been gardening in your present location for more than a couple of seasons. Try thinking back through the year to what your garden is like in any one season. It's important to think of positive as

~

An example of a typical house showing the planting potential of its various sides with notes on the conditions that each side is likely to experience.

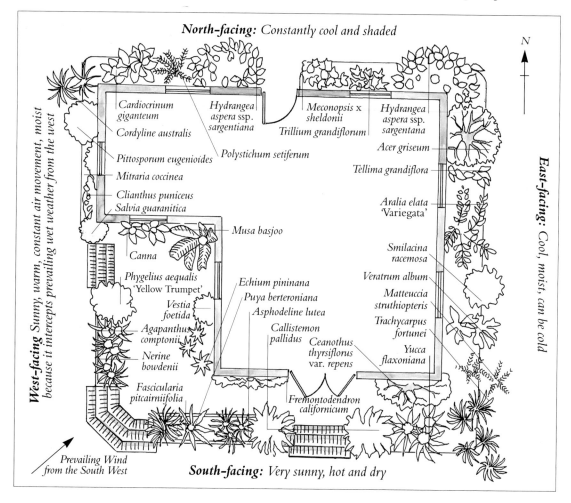

North-facing: *Constantly cool and shaded*

N

Cardiocrinum giganteum
Hydrangea aspera ssp. sargentiana
Meconopsis x sheldonii
Trillium grandiflorum
Hydrangea aspera ssp. sargentana
Acer griseum
Cordyline australis
Polystichum setiferum
Tellima grandiflora
Pittosporum eugenioides
Mitraria coccinea
Clianthus puniceus
Salvia guaranitica
Aralia elata 'Variegata'
Musa basjoo
Smilacina racemosa
Canna
Veratrum album
Phygelius aequalis 'Yellow Trumpet'
Echium pininana
Puya berteroniana
Matteuccia struthiopteris
Vestia foetida
Asphodeline lutea
Trachycarpus fortunei
Agapanthus comptonii
Callistemon pallidus
Ceanothus thyrsiflorus var. repens
Yucca flaxoniana
Nerine bowdenii
Fascicularia pitcairniifolia
Fremontodendron californicum

West-facing *Sunny, warm, constant air movement, moist because it intercepts prevailing wet weather from the west*

East-facing: *Cool, moist, can be cold*

Prevailing Wind from the South West

South-facing: *Very sunny, hot and dry*

The southwest corner of the previous diagram shows how the shelter of the building protects tender, hardy sun-loving and desert plants.

~

well as negative aspects. For example, a cold spot in winter may be a cool, moist location during summer and, similarly, a warm winter sun trap may be blisteringly hot during midsummer. It is also essential to consider seasonal weather changes in your local area which will help you enormously in building up a profile of what your garden's range of growing environments is like throughout the year.

Taking time to get to know your garden will make choosing the right position for new plants much easier and the following are some of the main points you should consider.

LENGTH OF SEASON

The length of the growing season will vary according to where you live (see maps on pages 125). Generally, the further north you are, the shorter the growing season. However, this can be misleading. For example, gardens in some large city centres can experience near sub-tropical conditions during summer with winters shortened because of the warmth produced by dense clusters of buildings.

Similarly, gardens on western coasts can be mostly frost-free because of the warming effect of the Gulf Stream. Other local factors, such as the way your garden faces, how exposed it is to strong or cold winds, whether it is in a small area where the frost lingers or several hundred feet above sea level on an exposed hillside, will also affect the length of your growing season. So, although we can generalize about the climate and the weather, local factors often mean that our gardens may experience extraordinary conditions which make every garden's growing environment unique.

ASPECT

This is one of the most important facts for any gardener to consider, especially first-time house buyers taking on a new garden. It's vital to know which way your garden faces. If you don't, ask the present owners a few simple questions, like: Where does the sun rise and set? Does the garden get much sun in winter? If so, for how long? And have a look at the bark of any existing trees. The side that has the most green algae on it is usually the north side.

The aspect of your garden will dictate to a certain degree the type of plants you can grow. If your garden is on a steep north-facing slope, it would be unrealistic to suggest that you could grow a range of tender, sun-loving plants successfully. But you might have just the right location for shade, and moisture-loving plants which would normally shrivel in a hot, dry sunny location. And knowing which of your house walls face south and west will be very important when growing tender plants, like *Sollya heterophylla* (Bluebell Creeper), that require the maximum amount of light and warmth in order to grow well. It's also important for hardy sun-loving plants, such as *Callistemon pallidus*, because they need ample warmth to ripen the current year's soft growth, which helps to prevent them from being damaged by winter frosts. While north-facing walls are shaded and cool during summer and provide excellent positions for hardy, but delicate foliage plants like *Hydrangea aspera* ssp. *sargentiana*.

If you have moved to a new house with an empty garden, it is a golden opportunity to place the plants in exactly the right location. With an established garden the best planting positions may already be taken by more common plants. You have to decide what to grow where and possibly take the bold step of removing some of the existing plants. This is not always easy for a novice gardener who may be reluctant to remove established plants.

RAINFALL

Ample and even rainfall is important for any garden, but the amount and frequency of rainfall your garden receives varies tremendously depending on where you live (see map on page 124). Generally, western and upland regions have more rainfall during the year with a large amount of this falling during summer. In contrast, eastern and lowland regions have less, often with long spells in summer when little or no rain falls at all. Here, soils in which moisture-loving plants are growing must not be allowed to dry out and regular applications of well-rotted organic matter are essential in sustaining adequate moisture. In areas with lower winter rainfall soils are often drier and saturation of plants' roots and crowns is less common. Dry conditions also mean that there is less water within the plants' stems and leaves, so there is less damage caused by internal ice formation during cold spells. Often tender plants will survive outside in these areas despite periods of cold weather simply because they are drier.

AIR MOVEMENT AND SHELTER

Extremes of air movement mean exposure to strong, cold or salt-laden winds which affect plant growth a lot. Of course, there is the physical damage that can occur to plants during storms and gales, but what is often overlooked is the slow continuous damage that takes place over a period of time. Even plants that are thought to be hardy can have their young foliage damaged by cold winds which may funnel down a particular part of your garden.

Air movement in your garden may be very different between the summer and winter: a sheltered location during summer may prove to be too exposed during winter, so when choosing a planting position you should consider how the air movement will vary over the whole year. Reducing the damaging effects of the winds in exposed gardens has to be a priority. This is best achieved by erecting a screen or windbreak, which can be man-made or living, such as a hedge. The most important point about windbreaks is that they must be permeable, allowing some air to pass through them. Without this permeability the wind is just forced over the top or around the sides, often causing damaging eddies and wind tunnels.

A brick wall or woven lap fence would create wind eddies (see illustration on page 14), whereas a partially open palisade or willow hurdle fence

~

The shade cast by the Trachycarpus fortunei *(page 63) in the background provides the perfect position for ferns like* Dryopteris dilatata *(page 89) below it.*

Solid barriers, such as fences and walls, left, can cause damaging turbulence. Hedges and shrubberies, above right, allow strong winds to permeate as well as reduce their ferocity.

~

would be more permeable to strong winds at the same time as reducing the instances of eddies. The same goes for hedging: a dense mass of conifers will be fairly impermeable, while a mixed hedge of evergreens and deciduous shrubs or an informal shrubbery will prove more effective as a windbreak. The objective is to slow down the wind not deflect it.

Wind damage, though, may not only be due to strong and cold winds. For example, a common problem with hardy Japanese maples is that their foliage shrivels during summer. This is not because they have been allowed to dry out, but because the situation they are in receives too much warm, dry air which dries out the foliage faster than the roots can replace moisture. Usually this occurs when they are grown in tubs or pots on a paved area with little or no shade and shelter to protect them. Placing them in a sheltered position with some dappled shade and away from wind tunnels often found between buildings should resolve this problem.

The same problem can occur with many woodland, variegated and delicate foliage plants. Woodlands normally have very constant conditions – diffused light, cool organic soil with abundant moisture all year round. Many woodland plants placed in the open border in full sun and exposure

Solid barriers at the base of slopes impair cold air drainage. On cold winter nights this can lead to the formation of a damaging frost pocket.

~

to free air movement will suffer because conditions there are contrary to their original sheltered home.

For anyone attempting to grow tender plants, cold winds can spell disaster since, as the wind speed increases, so does the wind chill factor. It's vital, therefore, that tender plants are positioned in the most sheltered part of the garden and consideration must be given to how exposed that area might be during winter. On exposed sites, a mixture of hardy, particularly evergreen, shrubs will be useful in shielding tender plants and maintaining a sheltered environment all year round.

Beware also of planting tender plants up against walls, fences or dense conifers at the base of a slope. On clear winter nights cold air will drain down the slope and collect up against the wall or other barrier, so creating a frost pocket which will damage the plants.

SUNLIGHT AND WARMTH

All plants appreciate sunlight and warmth in different degrees and if you are planning on cultivating tender plants, you should select a part of your garden that receives these two elements in large amounts. Sunlight is not only important for plant

growth, it is also needed to help plants initiate flower buds for the following year. This varies with individual plants: some require bright light coupled with warm days and cool nights in order to initiate flower buds properly, like *Fremontodendron californicum*. Quite often when gardeners complain that a plant they have been growing for a number of years will not flower, it means that it has been cultivated in conditions that are too shaded. The answer is either to move it to a better-lit position or to improve the light by pruning surrounding shrubs and overhanging branches. Of course this may not always be practical, especially if the branches are high up or in a neighbour's garden. If that is the case, it's probably best to relocate the plant.

Often hardy plants such as *Campsis radicans* (trumpet vine) are planted against warm sunny walls. This gives the false impression that they are tender, when in fact these favourable locations which provide ample warmth and light are helping to produce plant hormones that, in sufficient

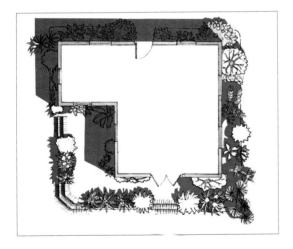

~

By noting the way the sun falls over your house and garden throughout the day, you can build up a picture of which areas are the sunniest and hottest and which are permanently shady. Here you see the shadows falling across a typical house at three different times of the day: 8.00 a.m. (left), midday (below left) and 4.00 p.m. (below).

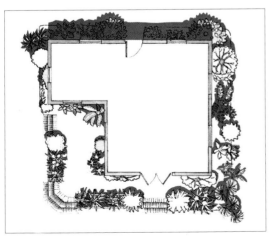

amount, will initiate new tissue to grow into next year's flower buds.

Some plants have a very high warmth and light requirement: if you planned to grow *Passiflora* x *caeruleoracemosa* then it would need warm sheltered conditions to grow well, but if you wanted it to flower and fruit, you should position it in a situation up against a south wall, for example, or in a sheltered courtyard where it would receive almost violent heat during the summer, otherwise buds would not be properly initiated for the following year's flowering.

Variegated plants do best in a well-lit position, but strong sunlight can burn young leaves and this, coupled with drying winds, can shrivel even the hardiest of variegated foliage. Their ideal planting location would be a part of the garden that only receives direct sun for part of the day, such as a border that faces west.

Warmth is of particular importance to plants from countries that experience hotter summers than our own. Often these plants, like *Salvia*

Looking away from the house, this typical suburban garden has some diverse planting positions, including a border shaded by fruit trees which is ideal for growing many of the shade-loving plants.

~

guaranitica, will come into growth in late spring and at the end of the year may still have a lot of soft growth on them. A warm sunny position ensures that the season is long enough to ripen the new growth properly, which is vital if it is not to be damaged by winter cold and the plant is to build up sufficient food reserves to last it through the winter.

SOILS AND MOISTURE LEVELS

Soils vary immensely from thin, shallow, alkaline soils over chalk to thick, deep, neutral brown earths in river flood plains and rich, organic, acidic, peaty soils in areas of high rainfall. Much has been written about soil cultivation and improvement and rightly so, as the soil is the most important constituent of any garden. All gardeners should get to

16

know their soil: digging a simple hole a couple of feet in depth will reveal how deep the top soil is and the condition of the underlying layers – the sub soil. You should also invest in a simple testing kit to find out what the pH balance of your soil is, because knowing whether your soil is very alkaline or slightly acidic will make a difference to the type of plants you can grow in it. But no soil should stop keen gardeners from growing the plants they desire. You can always provide tubs and containers for acid-loving plants in chalky areas and vice versa, but unless you want to be saddled with endless watering and feeding during summer, it's probably best to limit the amount of these.

Improving the soil is something the gardener has to work at continuously over a period of time. In established gardens it may have to be done at a fairly local level for individual borders and plants, while a new house with a garden presents a golden opportunity to cultivate the whole area thoroughly without the encumbrance of existing plants.

Try to work with your existing soil by altering it to meet the demands of your plants with the addition

Above: *Soil changes need not be to a whole border. They can be at a very local level, as shown here.*

~

Below: Hoheria glabrata *(see page 118) and* Eccremocarpus scaber aurantiacus *(see page 46) need shelter from winds and their heads in the sun.*

of different materials. For example, a rich clay soil might be ideal for most hardy herbaceous plants, but for ones requiring more drainage, like the lovely autumn-flowering *Nerine bowdenii*, the soil will have to be improved to provide better drainage. This can be done by adding grit and sand or one of the man-made soil improvers like perlite or vermiculite, mixed thoroughly into the top 30-50cm (12-20in) of soil before planting.

Organic matter is vital to any soil and improves soil drainage at the same time as increasing its water-holding capacity. It alters soil structure by helping the individual soil particles to stick together. These form larger clumps which hold more water and have bigger air spaces between them, allowing a freer passage of water down through the soil and more air in from the soil surface. However, any organic matter used must be well rotted, otherwise it will rob your soil of nitrogen whilst it continues rotting.

If your soil is totally unsuitable for the plant you wish to grow, then consider building a raised bed with a more suitable soil brought in from elsewhere. This is an excellent idea when perhaps only a few specimens need to be grown. Plants in raised beds also make fewer demands on watering time than those in pots. If, however, you garden on a heavy soil and wish to improve the drainage for one particular plant, be warned against choosing a part of the garden that is in a depression or at the base of a slope, or you may find that you have built yourself an unexpected soakaway which will fill with water during winter and drown your plants.

On free-draining sandy soils the reverse is often the norm. The emphasis here will be on retaining as much moisture in the soil during summer as possible. The incorporation of bulky organic matter deep down into the soil before planting and then mulching afterwards is the best way to achieve this. Plants like the *Gunnera manicata* (giant gunnera) will require a constant supply of summer moisture, so the more organic matter that can be provided, the better.

Soil fertility can vary, and some plants need a more fertile soil than others. Most heavy and alluvial (fine, fertile) soils tend to have a high nutrient content to start with, but many free-draining sands, gravelly soils and moist, peaty soils tend to be low in nutrients. For some plants, such as salvia, this is an advantage, as a rich soil would only encourage them to produce lush growth which may be susceptible to cold and disease, but most plants like a reasonably fertile soil. If your soil is weak, then you must improve it and this can be done in two ways: by adding either a bulky organic matter like garden compost or farmyard manure, or an artificial fertilizer. Personally, I tend to think it is best to use a combination of both. The bulky organics will improve the soil's structure, but when planting it is a good idea to add a little balanced fertilizer too. This could be a slow-release type or one of the organic soil improvers which could be used as a dressing to get the plants off to a really good start.

As a guide to how you should treat your soil, I have listed the five most common types below with some suggestions as to how you can deal with them.

Clay soil Often associated with poor drainage and difficult gardening conditions, clay soil needs careful handling. Trampling on the soil when it is wet can do far more damage than good, so avoid working on it if it is of a consistency which sticks to your boots and tools.

Improving this type of soil can be a long-term task. The key to success is organic matter which should be thoroughly mixed into all the layers of the top soil.

If your soil is very badly drained, then it may be a good idea to improve the drainage just in the vicinity of the plant you want to grow. Alternatively, you could construct a simple raised bed to keep the crown of the plant away from the waterlogged conditions. But don't be tempted just to dig a hole and fill it with stones as this will only create a soakaway which will fill with water during wet spells.

Sandy soil There is little problem with drainage in sandy soil as it is quite free-draining. But moisture retention can be poor, making it prone to drying out during the summer months. This often means that plants produce less lush growth. In the case of tender plants this can be an advantage since it means they are less likely to suffer from winter cold. Where excessive drying out is a problem, the moisture-holding capacity can be improved a lot by adding some well-rotted organic matter, such as farmyard manure, mushroom or garden compost, composted bark or wood chippings, leaf mould or even shredded paper. Incorporate it into the soil or use it as a mulch. Do make sure these materials really are well rotted and mixed in thoroughly with the top soil. Normally, this should be done during the dormant season – winter or early spring.

Chalky soil Shallow soils over chalk are notorious for drying out during the summer. Adding some organic matter can help conserve moisture levels, but it is important not to cultivate this type of soil too deeply otherwise the underlying chalk will be brought to the surface.

This sort of soil can be very alkaline (i.e., with a high pH level) which means that some plants find it difficult to take up certain nutrients, such as iron. You can recognize this problem by the leaves of the plant turning yellow (known as lime-induced chlorosis) and a reduction in the plant's growth. To remedy this, apply a little sequestrated iron solution as a foliar feed. Usually, however, the acids released from the rotting organic matter will reduce the soil's pH level, though beware of adding spent mushroom compost to chalky soils as it contains a fair amount of lime which can make the soil even more alkaline.

Peaty soil High in organic matter and acidic, peaty soil frequently occurs in areas of high rainfall and can often be boggy and wet for a large part of the year. This makes it rather difficult to grow tender plants. The best solution in this case is to construct a raised bed and add some better-draining soil to it, such as a sandy loam.

Alluvial soil Usually occurring in river valleys, this soil can make the best type of garden soil as it is well drained at the same time as being moisture-retentive and fertile. Certainly tender plants love alluvial soil. But it will always benefit from the addition of some organic matter, particularly when it is used as a mulch to help conserve summer moisture.

Don't feel you have to add vast quantities of improving material to your whole border just so that you can grow one plant. It makes more sense to concentrate your efforts on the area around the position of the plant – say, a square metre or so.

PESTS & DISEASES

At sometime or another your plants are likely to be infested with a pest or disease of some sort, whether it be aphids, whitefly or mealy bug, for example, or perhaps a fungus. There are varying opinions on whether to spray or not to spray. If I can avoid using chemicals I do, but sometimes it is necessary and it is better to spray at the first signs of pest or disease attack than when they are well established.

If you choose a chemical spray, it's important to make sure you pick the right type. A contact one (which will only kill the insects that are actually sprayed) containing pyrthrins/pyrethrum and resmethrin is useful for local pest problems, but for more serious infestations it is worth using a systemic spray (which will be absorbed into the plants' tissues and kill any insect feeding on the plant), such as dimethoate.

If you prefer, try an organic option. Soap solutions are good at controlling aphids and other winged pests, while more stubborn pests can be controlled by a liquid derris solution.

Diseases should be combatted first with a contact spray, like liquid copper, and later with a systemic fungicide such as benomyl. *Trichoderma viride* can be used as a biological control agent on certain fungi, such as silver leaf disease on prunus and other trees, but you may find you need a stronger one if the disease persists.

The other common pests that abound in any garden are slugs and snails. Really the most humane thing to do is to pick them off the plant and deposit them far away from your garden, but you may prefer to try a remedy recommended by your neighbours or other gardening friends, or if your garden is badly infested, you may have to resort to slug pellets.

Sunny Places

~

M ost gardens will have a warm, sunny spot or two, the ideal position for the plants in this section. Divided into three groups – tender, hardy sun-loving and desert – the plants featured come from some of the warmest parts of the world, such as Australia, California, the Mediterranean, Mexico, South Africa and South America, and they all share some basic needs for sun, warmth and a well-drained soil. As a result many plants from the three chapters can be mixed together to present interesting combinations. So, for example, many of the species from the Desert Plants chapter can be used as a focus amongst the tender and hardy sun-loving entries and need not necessarily be sited on their own. Do remember also that I have had to make certain distinctions between the plants in this section as to their hardiness for the purposes of dividing them into the three groups, but this may vary according to where you live.

For every plant you'll find here there are many more which could have been included, but the ones that are all have something particular to recommend them. Whether it be the striking pillars of *Echium pininana*, or the beautiful golden-yellow flowers of *Fremontodendron californicum*, or the tropical spiky leaves of *Agave americana*, you'll find that any one of these plants will add colour and shape to your garden, giving it a new and exotic touch. They are certainly some of my favourites and I hope will bring you as much pleasure.

~

Thriving in a warm sunny position, the tall multi-flowered heads of Agapanthus comptonii *(page 50) and the dark blue flowers of* Salvia guaranitica *(page 38) will bloom all summer long.*

Tender Plants

Many of our long-established garden plants, as well as a number of new and exciting species now available, originate from parts of the world where they experience very hot summers and predominantly mild, wet winters – places such as the Mediterranean, Mexico, California in the United States, South Africa and Australia. Among these are tender plants, that is those plants which are easily damaged by bad weather and unfavourable conditions and which are particularly susceptible to frost.

Since these plants frequently experience a long growing season in their native habitats, it won't come as a surprise that the plants in this chapter need a very sunny position in the garden with lots of warmth and shelter, especially from cold winds.

But tender plants are well worth growing. Their often delicate appearance and beautiful range of foliage and colourful flowers make them welcome additions to any garden.

SITE SELECTION

Every garden has the potential to grow some tender plants and when looking for the ideal position it is a good idea to start by examining the walls of your house or those which mark the boundaries of your garden.

A south- or west-facing wall is a particularly good place, but if you are unconvinced about how sheltered it might be, try placing your hands on the wall soon after sunset. If it has been a sunny day, the wall will feel warm and that heat will continue to radiate out through the night like a giant storage heater, helping to keep the plants against it warm and frost-free. During the growing season this warmth is vital to help growth ripen and so help the plants withstand the cold of winter. Of course, in the winter months the warmth that the wall absorbs will be much reduced, but it will still be enough to make a couple of degrees' difference between that situation and a position in a more open area, of the garden. In some cases this can

mean the difference between your plant's flowering and not flowering and even its life or death.

Although the shelter of a wall offers a good opportunity for growing tender plants, you could site them in a mixed shrub border which will also provide some protected areas. A mixture of evergreen and deciduous shrubs will help to break up strong winds and reflect the sun's energy on to the plants.

SOIL

The character of the soil is very important for growing tender plants successfully, with winter drainage being a key factor. Few of us have the ideal soil for these plants, but you can improve your soil in one of three ways:

1 By digging in lots of well-rotted organic matter, you can help the soil particles to stick together which in turn will form larger clusters and so allow air and water to pass between them. This improves the drainage around the plant and gives it a better chance to grow. If your soil has not had any organic matter added to it for several years, it may require several applications over a long period until you achieve the desired result.

2 If your soil is on the heavy side, it may be a good idea to add some sharp grit. For most plants, the addition of an amount equivalent to about half the soil in the planting area around the hole mixed into the top 30-50cm (12-20in) of soil should improve the drainage sufficiently. The best thing to do is to put the grit in when you are adding the organic matter.

3 Alternatively, you can add one of the man-made soil improvers, such as vermiculite or perlite in the same ratio as you would add the grit (see above). Again, these improvers will change the soil structure and its drainage for the better. The advantage of the soil improvers is that they are light in weight and therefore easy to transport. However, if you need a large amount, it can be expensive, whereas garden compost or other organic matter is often free.

For more information on improving soil see the first chapter, page 16.

PLANTING

It is always best to plant out tender plants in the late spring, after the threat of frosts has passed. They then have all summer to establish. Smaller specimens will establish themselves more quickly and successfully than larger ones and they can often grow to the same height in their first season. In colder areas, it is best to plant later on in early summer when the soil has warmed up. This gives tender plants less of a shock when transplanting.

Make sure you prepare the ground thoroughly beforehand. Mix in any additions to the soil well and do be certain that all the organic matter is well-rotted. Choose a dry day for this, when the soil is not too wet. If it doesn't stick heavily to your boots when you walk on it, then it's OK to start digging and forking.

If the plant you are putting in has been grown in a pot, tease out any roots that have become cramped at the bottom of the pot and spread them out in the planting hole. As a rough guide, the planting hole should be at least twice the size of the root ball so that there is sufficient room to spread the roots out properly.

Once you have put the plant in, backfill the hole carefully and firm the soil round the roots gently. Water the plant in well; this is especially important if the soil is already dry. If it is, you should also put some water in the bottom of the hole before you put the plant in.

Continue watering the new plants until they are established. How long this takes will depend on the season, but in summer the plants may need a good soaking every other day. Don't water little and often as this is counterproductive. It encourages surface rooting and also takes up a lot of time. When the plant has established, reduce the watering so as to encourage the roots to grow deep and search out their own supplies.

WINTER PROTECTION

If you live in a cold or fairly exposed area, your tender plants will almost definitely need some form of protection in the winter.

Mulching By far the cheapest method of protection is an insulation mulch. There are a variety to choose from, but there is one important factor to consider – the mulch must not become water-logged during the winter months. It is for this reason that peat and coir are unsuitable. One of the best insulators is straw, although this can look unsightly in the garden. I prefer to use chopped bracken which is light and lets the air in, but keeps the frost out, provided it is at least 30cm (1ft) thick. It can be held down by placing a piece of old pea netting over the top and pegging that down at the sides. Otherwise garden shreddings and coarse bark chips are effective when put over the crowns of tender plants, but do make sure that the bark shreddings really are coarse so as to allow the air to circulate and prevent the crowns from rotting.

Wrapping Wraps can be very effective as a form of insulation for tender plants. The best material to use is horticultural fleece. It is better than polythene because it lets the plant breath, whereas condensation can build up under polythene and that can lead to fungal problems. In very cold areas, it may be necessary to apply several layers to keep the cold out. Either wrap the fleece around the plant, or place it over the crown, or drape it over larger plants like a tent. Another alternative is to erect a simple frame over which you can place the fleece. This can prevent the plants from being damaged by the wind tugging at the fleece if it is directly on them.

Clianthus puniceus

(LOBSTER'S CLAW, PARROT'S BILL)

A superb evergreen shrub that really lives up to its name, *Clianthus puniceus* is grown for its glossy pinnate leaves and beautiful claw-shaped red flowers which appear in spring (see page 25). A native of New Zealand and a favourite of the Maoris, it can live up to 100 years, but in cultivation it's normally grown as a short-lived plant (usually lasting five to ten years) either outside in sheltered areas or in a cool conservatory. It occurs naturally in scrubland on rocky and sandy hills, and given good drainage and favourable conditions can prove hardy down to -10°C (14°F).

Eventually reaching a height of 2-2.5m (6-8ft) and a spread of 2.5m (8ft), *C. puniceus* looks good when planted with some interesting foliage shrubs, such as the purple cordyline (see page 53) or the silver *Helichrysum stoechas* and *H. italicum*, when its spring flowers are really set off to their best advantage.

CULTIVATION

Site Selection *C. puniceus* is best grown as a wall shrub trained against trellis or wires on a south- or southwest-facing wall. In more sheltered locations they can be grown up against a fence, but in either case it is very important that they have shelter from cold winds. On a south-facing wall they will tolerate some dappled shade from other shrubs. This can be very useful as they can be pruned to occupy the space lower down a wall which is often left bare by more mature shrubs and climbers. Full sun usually suits them best as it ensures that the sunlight reaches the base of the plant, so helping the protective winter mulch stay dry through the cold months.

Soil In their natural habitat clianthus have very free-draining soil. It's therefore essential that the soil they are planted in is well drained; this is particularly important during winter otherwise the plants will rot. Heavy soils must be improved (see page 22) and it is essential that any added improvers are thoroughly mixed into the existing soil to a depth of at least 30-50cm (12-20in). If you have a heavy clay soil, then it may be best to remove a sufficient amount from the area where the plant is to grow and to replace it (see illus. page 17). A suitable area would be 60 x 60cm (2 x 2ft). Where the soil is prone to waterlogging during wet periods and is slow to warm up during spring, it's probably best to grow the clianthus in a pot or container.

Planting Young plants are normally planted out in their final positions during late spring, after the threat of frosts has passed in well-prepared soil. If planting up against a wall, then the planting hole should be as close as possible to its base so that the plant really benefits from the shelter. The planting hole should be at least twice as big as the root ball. If it is needed, some fertilizer can be mixed into the soil at this stage. Plant the shrub at the same depth as it was in the pot. Don't firm the soil too hard around the new plant but make sure that it is in contact with the root ball and water the clianthus in well, even if rain is imminent.

AFTERCARE

Feeding Clianthus don't need a lot of feeding, so they thrive in most soils. But a light sprinkling of some slow-release general fertilizer around the base of the shrub during spring is a good idea and then, about once a month through the growing season, from spring to the end of summer, they can be given a liquid feed – one which is high in potash rather than nitrogen which would stimulate too much soft growth.

Pruning Pruning usually takes place in early summer after the flowers have faded. Remove any dead, diseased or weak growths and prune the shrub to form a flowering frame for next year's blooms. It's best to tie new growths into the training wires, since this ensures that the plant will be growing up against the wall where it will benefit from the additional reflected warmth.

Winter Protection In all but the mildest localities clianthus will need some winter protection. By far the best is a thick dry mulch put around the base of the shrub in the autumn. This should be at least 25cm (10in) thick and be composed of either dry leaf mould, chopped straw or bracken – both the latter benefit from being covered and pegged down with pea netting to prevent the wind from blowing them away. In cold districts clianthus are usually cut down to ground level by frost during winter, but with the correct protective mulch they should regenerate each spring.

Clianthus puniceus is best grown against a warm sheltered wall where its branches can be trained.

~

Pests & Diseases Clianthus are relatively free of pests and diseases, but under glass they can be prone to attack from mealy bug and red spider mite. (See page 19 for solutions).

PROPAGATION

You can propagate by seed sown in spring in an open gritty compost which should be maintained at 15-18°C (60-65°F). Seed normally germinates within one month. Alternatively, semi-ripe cuttings taken in summer from the new season's growth will root easily in a closed case with bottom heat. Once rooted, the plants can be potted up into an open, gritty, loam-based compost and watered moderately during the growing season, but sparingly during autumn and winter.

OTHER VARIETIES

C. puniceus 'Albus' H & S: 2 x 1.5m (6 x 5ft). It has similar flowers that are white tinged with green. *C. puniceus* 'Flamingo' H & S: 2 x 1.5m (6 x 5ft). Attractive with dark glossy green leaves and deep rose-pink flowers. *C. puniceus* 'Red Admiral' H & S: 2.5 x 2m (8 x 6ft). This has bright red flowers in large numbers. All varieties bloom in the spring.

Vestia foetida

(VESTIA)

An attractive free-flowering evergreen shrub from Chile, *Vestia foetida* deserves better recognition. During early summer it's covered in butter-yellow tubular flowers which have a star-shaped opening at the end (see page 53). Being upright in habit, it makes a useful plant for the middle or back of the border. As the species name suggests, the foliage is rather malodorous and it's a member of the potato family so all green parts and especially the seeds are poisonous and should not be eaten.

V. foetida tolerates temperatures down to -10°C (14°F), but will regrow after colder spells. It looks great when planted with *Phygelius aequalis* 'Yellow Trumpet' (see page 43) and other sun-loving plants like *Verbena bonariensis*.

CULTIVATION

Site Selection Vestia require a warm sunny position on a well-drained soil. In sheltered localities they can be grown in the open border, but in cooler areas they do best with the protection of a warm wall. They must have shelter from cold winds otherwise the foliage will blacken and shrivel. In very cold regions it may be better to grow the vestia in a container so that it can be placed outside in a sunny position during the growing season and brought indoors in winter.

Soil Vestia prefer a well-drained soil, but they will grow on heavy soils provided they do not become waterlogged. Dig over the soil thoroughly and, if necessary, you can add a small amount (about the equivalent of a quarter of the surrounding soil) of well-rotted organic matter, like spent mushroom compost or stable manure, to the top 40cm (16in) to improve the soil structure.

Planting It's always best to plant young vigorous specimens of about one to two years of age. This is normally done in spring after the threat of frosts has passed, but they can be planted at any time during the growing season. When planting against a wall, place the plant about 25cm (10in) from it. The vestia has a strong upright branch network, so this space allows some branches to develop between the stem and the wall. Young plants are prone to wind throw and may need staking until established.

If you grow these plants in containers, use a loam-based soil, such as John Innes No 3. Vestia don't thrive in soil-less composts such as peat or coir, so avoid them. Do note that mature plants need a lot of water.

AFTERCARE

Feeding Since vestia are not heavy feeders, they thrive in most soils. Excessively limy or chalky soils may cause foliage to yellow, but this can be rectified with an application of sequestrated iron or a balanced fertilizer. Plants normally respond quickly to fertilizer, so if a dressing is applied during spring it need only be used sparingly.

Pruning Plants require only light pruning, which is usually done in late spring to remove any winter-damaged shoots. Established plants can grow quickly and may need the occasional prune to bring them back into shape. Avoid pruning in the middle of winter.

Winter Protection In most regions vestia will survive all but the coldest of winters outside. In areas that would normally expect cold winters, though, improving the soil drainage is very important, as plants that are kept drier at the roots are far more likely to survive. The base of the plant can also be mulched with leaf mould, or chopped straw or bracken to a depth of 25cm (10in).

Pests & Diseases Although relatively free of pests and diseases, vestia can sometimes suffer from infestations of aphids. (See Pests & Diseases, page 19).

PROPAGATION

Vestia germinate easily from seed sown under glass in the spring and kept at 15-18°C (60-65°F). Seedlings reach flowering age in their second year. Alternatively, cuttings taken from green wood during the summer and placed in a propagator with gentle bottom heat root easily. And semi-ripe cuttings taken in early autumn and inserted into a cutting frame outside will be rooted by the following spring.

OTHER VARIETIES

There is one other variety of vestia in cultivation which is a white form, *V. lycioïdes*, but I do not recommend it. Its flowers are a poor quality white and I think it is an inferior plant to the yellow-flowered variety.

Sollya heterophylla

(BLUEBELL CREEPER, AUSTRALIAN BLUEBELL)

A delightful twining, semi-evergreen climber native to western Australia, *Sollya heterophylla* is really rewarding to grow with its small, but gracefully nodding, bell-shaped, sky-blue flowers which are produced in large numbers from summer through to autumn (see page 28). It can reach a maximum height of 1.5-2.1m (5-7ft) and a spread of 90-120cm (3-4ft) and will tolerate temperatures of as low as -4°C(25°F), provided the stems have been well-ripened the previous summer.

Sollya look good climbing through other shrubs such as pittosporum (see page 30) and *Olearia virgata* or over a fence or through other climbers like *Passiflora* x *caeruleoracemosa* (see page 29).

CULTIVATION

Site Selection Sollya can be grown outside in the mildest of localities, provided they are planted in a sheltered position. They do best in full sun, but will tolerate part-shade. They are usually grown as a wall shrub and the thin twining nature of the stems means sollya are best trained either up netting or through other shrubs. Ideally, they need to be planted against a warm, sunny south- or south-west-facing wall or in a sheltered sunny courtyard. Wherever the location, it must be away from cold north and easterly winds.

Soil The soil should be well drained at the same time as being moisture-retentive and humus-rich. Sollya will grow on dry gravelly and gritty soils, but the plants' growth and performance are much reduced. A gritty loam mixed in a 2:1 ratio with some well-rotted garden compost, leaf mould or chopped bark will be best. If grit or vermiculite are needed to improve the drainage, then they should also be added in a 1:2 ratio. Anything that is added to the garden soil should be carefully mixed into a planting area of 50cm (20in) in diameter and 40-50cm (16-20in) deep. If your soil is extremely wet and heavy then it's probably best to plant sollya in a raised bed or container. For growing them in a container, use a soil-based compost, such as John Innes No. 3, with a third of chopped bark or coir added.

Planting Young specimens are normally planted out during spring after the threat of frosts has passed. If planting against a wall, put the plant within 15cm (6in) of the wall to benefit from any reflected heat. When planting under a shrub in a mixed border, take care not to select a shrub that casts too heavy a shade.

Generally when planting it is a good idea to give the soil a light dressing of a slow-release fertilizer or an organic equivalent that is not high in nitrogen or the plant will put on too much soft growth. All plants should be planted at the same depth as they were in their pots and watered in well. This is particularly important when planting up against a warm wall as this area sometimes does not receive direct rainfall, because of overhanging roofs. Watering must be thorough and frequent – every other day in hot spells – until the plant is established. Then it can be reduced until it's no longer required.

AFTERCARE

Feeding Sollya don't need a lot of nutrition, so avoid heavy applications of fertilizer. If you grow them in a container, however, you can apply a general liquid fertilizer through the growing season.

Pruning Pruning is normally carried out during spring to remove dead and weak growths. Because of the tangled nature of the plant, pruning can be difficult and should be done carefully to avoid cutting the wrong shoot. When pruning a new or potted plant, pinch out shoots to encourage branching. Strong leading growths can be trained up wires or around hoops and the subsequent lateral shoots can be pruned to short spurs of 15cm (6in). This will form a bushy plant around a predetermined frame.

Winter Protection In sheltered localities sollya will survive outside without any winter protection, but in colder districts they may require some simple cover, such as horticultural fleece, which should be doubled and placed over the plant and secured to

Tender evergreen shrubs like Pittosporum eugenioïdes, *left and inset (page 30), can be used as a support for climbers like the sky-blue-flowered* Sollya heterophylla *and the flamboyant* Passiflora x caeruleoracemosa *with its show-stopping flowers.*

~

the wall. This can either be left on for the winter or just put on during cold spells. You can also mulch the base of the plant with chopped bracken or straw. If wrapped plants seem unsightly, then only the bottom 30cm (12in) need be protected since established plants will almost always sprout from ground level if the upper branches are killed during winter. Plants in containers can be taken into a cool greenhouse or conservatory until early spring. During winter they should be watered sparingly, but not allowed to dry out completely.

Pests & Diseases Almost free of pests and diseases outside, sollya can be prone to attack from red spider mite and aphids under glass.(See page 19.)

PROPAGATION

Seed is usually sown in spring in an open gritty compost with the temperature maintained at 21°C (70°F). However, germination can be erratic, so you may have more success with soft heeled or soft wood cuttings which can be taken in early summer. They are best rooted in a closed case or propagator with bottom heat and should be shaded until rooted.

OTHER VARIETIES

S. heterophylla 'Alba' H & S: 2.1 x 1.5m (7 x 5ft). This is a most attractive plant with white flowers, especially when planted in amongst the normal blue form. *S. parviflora* H & S: 2.1 x 1.5m (7 x 5ft). This has more slender shoots and darker blue flowers, but it is much less common.

Passiflora x caeruleoracemosa

(PASSION FLOWER)

Passiflora are a group of mainly evergreen climbing plants with exquisitely beautiful flowers, attractive foliage and colourful, edible fruits. *Passiflora x caeruleoracemosa* is a delightful hybrid which looks good growing up walls and it really needs a sheltered area, preferably one that is close to a building. Its stunning large purple flowers with white-tipped filaments appear during summer and can reach between 10-13cm (4-5in) in diameter (see opposite).

Most passiflora originate from South America and are frost-tender and *P. x caeruleoracemosa* is hardy down to -2°C (29°F) and behaves herbaceously in the garden, whereas inside it is evergreen. A strong-growing plant, it can reach a height of 3m (10ft) and a spread of 2m (6ft) in one year.

P. x *caeruleoracemosa* looks attractive when planted with *Sollya heterophylla* (see page 27).

CULTIVATION

Site Selection This hybrid needs warmth to thrive and so should be planted against a south- or south-west-facing wall where it can bask in the sunshine. Ensure the planting position is in full light as passifloras don't like permanent shade. They will tolerate some shade but only for a short time. Shelter is important, particularly from strong winds which tend to damage young shoots. However, when shoot tendrils have clasped their support they are impossible to remove without breaking them.

Soil Drainage, especially during the winter dormant period, is vital, but in summer ample moisture is needed to sustain growth. A special kind of mix is therefore essential. It's best to provide maximum drainage in the immediate vicinity of the plant and a mixture of coarse gravel or old builders' rubble will do very well. Problems with heavy soil can be overcome by creating a raised bed, while the underlying soil should also be improved by adding an equal part of either sharp grit or a man-made soil improver. Passiflora dislike a rich soil which only induces soft growth and soils with a high pH balance may cause lime-induced chlorosis which can yellow the leaves. This can be corrected by the addition of sequestrated iron.

Planting This is normally done during late spring or early summer when the fear of frosts has passed or throughout the growing season if necessary. When plants have been grown in a 100 per cent organic compost, I try and tease some of this away from young plants because during winter this compost will act like a sponge, absorbing water and causing rot problems. Water new plants in well.

AFTERCARE

Feeding Passiflora in general originate on poor sandy soils and so do not require high levels of nutrients. Young plants will benefit from a light occasional liquid feed in spring, but plants grown in containers will require more regular feeding – once a week throughout the growing season with a general balanced fertilizer.

Pruning Passiflora are best pruned in the late spring when any dead growth can be removed. Herbaceous plants can be pruned to 45cm (18in) in the autumn and cut back again during the spring to live wood. During the growing season plants should be allowed to grow as freely as possible as new growth bears the flowers.

Winter Protection Plants grown outside should be heavily insulated with either straw or bracken to a depth of 45cm (18in). This can then be covered with a sheet of polythene which should preferably stretch at least 45cm (18in) away from the base of the plant. It will help to deflect rainwater away from the roots, keeping them dry and frost-free under their mulch. If growing passiflora up a wall, frame lights can be placed at an angle against the wall to deflect the rain. Insulation should be packed underneath to ensure a frost-free environment.

Pests & Diseases Aphids can be a problem on young growth in spring, and fungal wilt disease can mean trouble as it is indicative of poor soil drainage and poor root growth. Symptoms such as rapid yellowing of the foliage show that it's too late to save the plant. Drench the soil with a fungicide solution and site new plants in a different location.

PROPAGATION

Passiflora can be raised from seed. Germination from fresh seed is rapid, but dried seed can take up to twelve months and should be kept at 21-27°C (70-80°F). Cultivars are normally raised from softwood and semi-ripe cuttings which root easily, especially if given a hormonal root dip, although this is not essential. Tip cuttings from lateral shoots can be taken from summer through to early autumn and should be 10-15cm (4-6in) long. Herbaceous species can be propagated from 10-cm (4-in) root cuttings taken in spring. Pot them near to the surface of the compost and keep them at 21°C (70°F). New plants can also be successfully raised from layering.

OTHER VARIETIES

P. caerulea H & S: 4 x 2m (12 x 6ft). Perhaps the most common and popular of passionflowers, this vigorous evergreen climber produces blue and white flowers in summer through to autumn when egg-shaped fruits appear, turning orange when ripe. *P.* 'Incense' H & S: 3 x 2m (10 x 6ft). This cultivar, which was introduced from America in an attempt to breed more hardiness in to passiflora, is another herbaceous species. It produces stunning large purple flowers during summer.

Pittosporum eugenioïdes
(LEMONWOOD TREE)

One of an extremely beautiful group of small evergreen trees and large shrubs, *Pittosporum eugenioïdes* gets its common name from the aromatic smell of its crushed foliage. This species can grow to an average of 4m (12ft) in sheltered locations with a spread of 2-2.5m (6-8ft). It is particularly handsome

with untypically long leaves of up to 10cm (4in) which are dark glossy green with a black midrib and held on black stems (see page 28). Bearing small yellow-green and honey-scented flowers in spring, the whole plant shines in bright sunlight and looks particularly attractive when planted next to variegated and silver-foliaged plants like *P. tenuifolium* 'Silver Queen' and *Convolvulus cneorum*. (see page 59). In fact the whole genus is noted for its attractive foliage which varies from dark purple-bronze to apple green and some variegated forms.

P. eugenioïdes prefers a sheltered situation away from cold winds. It is hardy down to -5°C (23°F), but will tolerate this for only a short time.

CULTIVATION

Site Selection Pittosporum are best grown outside in a warm sunny position in any well-drained soil. They are particularly suitable for coastal planting, being tolerant of salt spray and thriving in the maritime climate where they can reach 5m (15ft), and make excellent hedging plants either clipped or as an informal screen. Best grown against a sheltered west wall or in a warm sheltered corner of the garden, in cold districts they can be grown under glass and stood outside during summer.

Soil Soils must be well drained. Heavy soils should be broken up and organic matter dug in to improve the structure. They do not do well on thin alkaline soils. When growing pittosporum in a pot or container, use a soil-based John Iinnes No. 3 with one part added coir.

Planting Pittosporum are normally planted in the spring after the danger of frost has passed, though they can be planted at any time during the summer, providing they are well watered in and receive some shade until they have settled. Young plants are normally staked for the first couple of years until they have established a strong root system. At planting time a small dressing of an organic fertilizer sprinkled into the planting hole will help to stimulate root activity. Continue to water the plant until it is well established.

AFTERCARE

Feeding Pittosporum require very little feeding in the garden. But container-grown plants will appreciate a weekly liquid feed during the growing season and repotting once every season.

Pruning All pittosporum are tolerant of pruning, whether clipping to form a hedge or more formative pruning to keep large shrubs to a desired shape and size. This can be done at any time during the late spring or early summer.

Winter Protection As *P. eugenioïdes* eventually attains a large size, winter protection can be difficult. The important point is to site the plant in the best position in the first instance. If a shrub has to be protected, it's best covered in horticultural fleece held down by stones to prevent it blowing away. Around the base of the shrub the ground should be mulched with dry bracken or straw to prevent the roots from freezing.

Pests & Diseases These plants suffer few pests and diseases, except scale insect, which can be a problem when plants are grown under glass.

PROPAGATION

Seed is best sown fresh in autumn or early spring and maintained at a temperature of 21°C (70°F). Cultivars are normally increased by cuttings. These are best taken as 10-cm (4-in) semi-ripe basal cuttings in summer. They root easily if inserted into a propagator with bottom heat and kept at 16-18°C (60-65°F). Alternatively, take ripe basal cuttings in late autumn and insert into a cold frame. These will normally root by late the following spring.

OTHER VARIETIES

P. tenuifolium 'James Stirling' H & S: 3 x 2m (10 x 6ft). Has small silver-green leaves with wavy margins, and stems that are black tinged with red. It produces small, brown, honey-scented flowers in spring. *P. tenuifolium* 'Purpureum' H & S: 3 x 2m (10 x 6ft). Has foliage with wavy margins that turns purple-bronze as the leaves age. *P. undulatum* H & S: 2.5 x 2m (8 x 6ft). Its long, glossy, dark green leaves have wavy margins and the flowers produced in late spring or early summer are creamy-white and fragrant. Only suitable for the mildest localities.

Musa basjoo
(JAPANESE BANANA)

A dramatic plant even when young, *Musa basjoo* is primarily grown for its foliage. One leaf can reach 2m (6ft) long, and is apple green with an attractive dark midrib (see page 32). Its flowers are small and appear in spring within yellow-green bracts. In warm conditions *M. basjoo* will produce small yellow-green fruit, just like little bananas of about 6 x 2.5cm (2½ x 1 in) which have white flesh. The Japanese banana, as it is called, originates from the Ryuku Islands at the southern tip of Japan. It is one of the toughest species, but still requires warm temperatures and abundant moisture for growth. However, *M. basjoo* will grow at a minimum temperature of 12°C (54°F). Winter frosts will kill the foliage, but the underground rhizome will tolerate short frosts of -5°C (23°F) and with winter protection plants will regenerate in spring and soon attain its former size. In extremely sheltered localities it may be grown outside all year, providing it is well prepared for winter dormancy.

In northern climates it can reach a height of 4m (12ft) and a spread of 3m (10ft). It looks best with cordyline (see page 53) and *Trachycarpus fortunei* (see page 63).

CULTIVATION

Site Selection Musa need as much warmth as they can be given. An extremely sheltered southwest- or south-facing part of the garden away from any cold winds suits them best. Strong winds will reduce growth and have the destructive effect of shredding the leaves. If the plants are to be left outside during winter, consider a location up against the shelter of a building or glasshouse. Alternatively, I lift the plants in autumn, remove the foliage and pot up the root ball and place them in a frost-free greenhouse or conservatory.

Soil The ideal soil is a deep, fertile loam with adequate amounts of organic matter. Thin or poor soils can be improved by the addition of one third well-rotted manure or garden compost, thoroughly mixed into the top 45cm (18in). Where neither of these two materials is available, then substitute chopped bark, coir or mushroom compost. To improve the fertility of these materials add a nine-month slow-release fertilizer. For plants grown in pots, use a soil-based compost, such as John Innes No. 3 with one third of chopped bark or coir. Repot annually in the spring.

Planting Outside planting is normally done in the late spring when the threat of frosts has passed and the soil has warmed up. Fork the soil over before planting to allow the air to get in.

Young plants should be put out when they are in active growth, so make sure that plants which have been overwintered indoors have started to grow again. This is evidenced by the emergence of new leaves from the top of the plant and new white fleshy roots from the rhizome. Apply a dressing of slow-release fertilizer into the planting hole and water plants in well – a weak solution of seaweed extract helps to stimulate root activity. A 15-cm (6-in) mulch of bark, garden or mushroom compost should be applied around the plants to help retain soil moisture and suppress weeds. These dark mulches will absorb the energy from the sun and help to warm the soil, so promoting faster root growth. And they will alleviate any compaction of the soil that may have occurred during winter.

AFTERCARE

Feeding During the growing season musa grow rapidly and require a weekly feed of either organic liquid manure or an artificial equivalent. Providing the soil has been well prepared and a slow-release fertilizer has been added at planting time, there should be no need to apply any additional fertilizer other than a liquid feed.

Pruning Musa require very little pruning. As the plant grows older, leaves fade and these can be removed when they turn yellow. Established plants may flower and when this happens root growth will cease while the plant puts all its energy into fruiting and seed development. Afterwards the stem withers and dies. Towards the end of this period new shoots will appear at the base, two of which should be allowed to grow. When one reaches 45cm (18in), remove the weaker of the two.

~

Opposite: *Bold foliage effects can be achieved by planting the banana plant,* Musa basjoo, *to the left of the picture, with the giant-leaved* Gunnera manicata *(page 83). They are seen here with the orange-flowered lily,* Canna x generalis *(see page 41).*

Right: *The orange-flowered* Mitraria coccinea *(page 34) and the dark evergreen* Myrtus communis *(page 35), to the left of it, both need a sheltered corner in which to grow well.*

Winter Protection Plants left outside during winter must be protected against cold and wet or they will rot. Normally frost will cut the upper parts of the plant down. Alternatively, you can remove leaves in mid autumn before the first frosts arrive. Mulch plants with a layer of dry bracken or straw that is at least 60cm (2ft) deep and wrap polythene over the mulch and around the stem – a simple frame of canes, polythene and string will keep the rain off and help to deflect moisture away from the base of the plant. This wrapping should stay on until the threat of frosts has passed.

Plants that are lifted should be potted up into a mixture of chopped bark and coir which should be kept only slightly moist through the dormant period.

Pests & Diseases Musa are generally trouble free when grown outside, but lifted plants might need the occasional fungicide application to discourage moulds during the dormant period.

PROPAGATION

Musa grow quickly when propagated from seed. This is sown in spring and germinates at 21°C (70°F), Seed compost should be moisture-retentive and free-draining: a mixture of 50 per cent coir and vermiculite kept evenly moist suits them best. Plants raised from seed grow quickly and are quite often large enough to plant into their final pot size at the end of their second growing season. Plants can also be divided, but it is important to ensure that each division has a portion of rhizome which will produce new roots. Division is normally done in the autumn, if the plants are lifted, or in spring when the plants are showing signs of growth.

OTHER VARIETIES

M. velutina H & S: 1.5 x 1.5m (5 x 5ft). Its handsome leaves are dark green above with a red midrib beneath. This species will require a minimum temperature of 16°C (60°F) to grow well, so it should be overwintered indoors. *M. acuminata* (formally *M. cavendishii*) 'Dwarf Cavendishii' H & S: 1.5 x 2m (5 x 6ft). A small form of the commercially-grown banana, it has broad leaves and will flower and bear fruit when grown under glass. It can be grown successfully in a large container.

Mitraria coccinea

(MITRE FLOWER)

A delightful little evergreen plant from Chile with a height of only 40cm (16in) and a spread of 30cm (12in), *Mitraria coccinea* produces small, tubular, bristly flowers which are a stunning orange-scarlet and which appear in flushes from spring through to late summer (see page 33). When in flower the whole bush glistens with vivid blossoms set against dark green foliage. It is ideal for a sheltered spot in part shade on the rock garden under a shrub or small tree. And it can also be grown in a pot or container. Since it is an acid-loving plant, it looks good in a peat bed with other ericaceous plants like *Desfontainia spinosa* and *Agapetes serpens*. Mitraria are hardy down to -5°C (23°F), but prefer that the temperature does not fall below freezing too often.

CULTIVATION

Site Selection Mitraria prefer cool moist conditions during the growing season in a location that does not get too cold during winter. In the garden they are best planted in a sheltered spot with a west- or southwest-facing aspect and they prefer part-shade either in the form of dappled light or shade for part of the day. Given ideal conditions in warmer climates, these plants may clamber over mossy tree trunks.

Soil A cool, moist, humus-rich soil suits them best. They dislike alkaline conditions and prefer a neutral or acidic soil. In the garden these conditions can be created by coir or leaf mould added to the soil in equal measures, or the provision of a specially made soil consisting of one part coir, one part chopped bark and one part sandy loam.

For potting compost the same mix can be used but the sandy loam can be substituted with John Innes Potting Compost No. 3.

Planting Planting normally takes place in the spring after the danger of frosts has passed. The soil should be prepared so that it is has a high organic content as described above. When planting, give new plants a general dressing of fertilizer to stimulate them into growth. Plants should be planted at the same depth as they were in their pot and watered in well. Staking is not normally necessary, but taller varieties planted next to a trellis or netting may require tying in to prevent them from flopping.

AFTERCARE

Feeding Mitraria require little feeding, but on soils that prove too alkaline they can soon reveal signs of iron deficiency which shows up as yellowing in between the leaf veins. This can be corrected by monthly applications of sequestrated iron solution. During the growing season they also appreciate fortnightly feeds with a liquid fertilizer high in potash.

Pruning The occasional light prune is necessary in spring to remove any weak or dead shoots that may have died during winter. Shoots that have flowered heavily may be cut down to new growth during the growing season, otherwise pruning is only necessary to keep plants in shape.

Winter Protection In favourable locations plants can be left outside with little or no protection, but in colder districts they will need some insulation. A layer of light, dry, one-year-old leaf mould topped with chopped bracken is best, held down with netting. In cold weather the top growth is often killed, but covered stems will reshoot the following spring. In very cold districts plants can be lifted and overwintered in a greenhouse.

Pests & Diseases Few pests and diseases trouble mitraria. Vine weevil occasionally infests potted plants and in spring aphids can be a problem on young growth (see page 19).

PROPAGATION

Seed is very fine, like dust, and is best sown in the spring. It should only be covered with a pane of glass and kept at 21°C (70°F). In part-shade germination occurs within eight weeks. Cuttings taken from late spring to the end of summer of soft-wood or semi-ripe material are the most successful way to increase plants. Given a dip in a rooting hormone, they will establish quickly. Stems that fall to the ground will also root sometimes and should be lifted and given sheltered conditions until fully established. But this method is slower to produce new plants than root cuttings from new material.

OTHER VARIETIES

M. coccinea 'Lake Puye' H & S: 1.5 x 1.25m (5 x 4ft). It is ideal for growing against a wall or up trellis and has a long flowering season, producing 4-cm (1½ in) bristly, orange flowers.

Myrtus communis

(MYRTLE)

An extremely handsome evergreen shrub or small tree which grows to a height of 5m (15ft) and spreads to about 3m (10ft), *Myrtus communis* has beautiful glossy and deliciously aromatic foliage (see page 33) which has long been prized for wedding bouquets because it was held sacred to the goddess of love by the Greeks and Romans. It produces sweetly fragrant flowers in spring followed by small blue-black berries in autumn. A versatile shrub which can be clipped into topiary forms or formal hedges, myrtus also does well as an informal screen. Given good drainage and shelter, it will tolerate temperatures between -10°C (14°F) and -15°C (5°F) and their tolerance of strong salt-laden winds makes them ideal for coastal planting where in mild localitiesthey

CULTIVATION

Site Selection Myrtus generally prefer a sheltered position in full sun away from cold winds. In cold districts they should be grown against a south- or southwest-facing wall, either as informal shrubs or trained as espaliers. If your garden is in an area that experiences long hard frosts, then it is best to grow them in pots and bring them indoors during the winter. In fact, pot culture enables the plants to be easily transported and they are often cut into shapes and placed in prominent areas of the garden during summer.

Soil Myrtus prefer a moderately fertile, well-drained, humus-enriched soil. They dislike heavy clay, but are tolerant of alkaline conditions. Soils should be enriched with leaf mould, garden compost or shredded bark thoroughly worked into the top 45 cm (18in) before planting.

For growing myrtus in pots, use a loam-based compost, like John Innes No. 2, with one third of shredded bark added. This should be watered moderately during the growing season and just kept moist during the dormant season.

Planting Planting normally takes place in the spring, but potted plants can be planted out at any time during the growing season, provided they are watered in well and not allowed to dry out. In exposed coastal gardens young plants may need some protection from strong winds until they are established.

AFTERCARE

Feeding A slow-release general fertilizer applied during spring will help to stimulate strong growth on new plants. Established plants rarely need feeding. Plants in pots can be fed with a liquid manure fortnightly during the growing season, but this should be stopped when growth slows down towards autumn. A slow-release fertilizer can also be added to the compost at potting time.

Pruning Pruning is only needed to keep plants in shape, but occasionally a dead branch or straggly shoots may need to be removed. When myrtus are grown as a hedge or as topiary forms, pruning can take place after the first flush of growth in late spring. Plants may also need a second cut at the end of the summer.

Winter Protection Provided they are planted in the right location, myrtus need very little winter protection except a thick dry mulch of chopped bracken around the base of the plant to prevent prolonged frost from freezing the roots.

Pests & Diseases Myrtus are generally trouble free, although mealy bug and scale insect can affect plants when they are grown under glass.

PROPAGATION

Propagation is normally done by cuttings – either semi-ripe nodal cuttings taken in summer and rooted in sharp sand in a closed shaded frame or a propagator with bottom heat; or by basal cuttings of the current year's growth taken in late autumn and rooted over winter in a frost-free cold frame.

Seed is normally sown in spring, the seeds being extracted from their berries and washed before sowing. They should be kept at 21°C (70°F) until germination occurs.

OTHER VARIETIES

As a genus of plants, *Myrtus* has attracted the attention of the taxonomists more than once, with the result that there are now only two species in the genus and plants previously found under this genus are now classified under *Lophomyrtus* and *Ugni*. M.

communis ssp. *tarentina (*Tarentum Myrtle) H & S: 3 x 2m (10 x 6ft). It is a hardier form with a compact, rounded habit and has narrow, needle-like leaves and creamy-white fragrant flowers. *M. communis* 'Microphylla' H & S: 2 x 1.25m (6 x 4ft). This has dark green leaves and white flowers. It is ideal if space is limited or for cultivation in a container.

Echium pininana
(GIANT ECHIUM)

One of the most striking biennial plants there is, *Echium pininana* grows to a single-stemmed, strong, upright plant of 1.5m (5ft) in height and spreads to 1m (3ft) with coarse leaves up to 45cm (18in) long in its first year. Flowering then takes place in the second or third year when the echium sends up a tall spike of about 3-4m (10-12ft) with thousands of small violet-purple flowers which fade to cerise (see opposite). Towards the end of summer the flower spike can be as much as 4m (12ft) high and looking up through a flowering group of echium is similar to looking up through the pillars of a cathedral. This dramatic effect is put to good use when they are planted in a group in the mixed border with other sun-loving perennials, like salvia (see page 38), pittosporum (see page 30) and myrtus (see page 35). A native of the Canary Isles, the echium is hardy down to -3°C (27°F) for short periods of time.

CULTIVATION

Site Selection Echium need a warm sheltered location away from cold winds and a west- or southwest-facing situation is best. Near the coast they are well able to withstand exposure to coastal breezes and salt-laden winds. Inland they are best planted up against the shelter of a building or in a sunny courtyard.

Soil It is particularly important that echium don't get waterlogged, so the soil has to be well drained. They appreciate moisture during the summer, but also show remarkable drought tolerance. A sandy loam with added grit which is moderately fertile

Few plants match the cathedral-like spires of Echium pininana *which grow up to 4m (12ft) high to meet the sunlight.*

~

suits them best. Heavy soil should either be removed and replaced with a suitable mixture or improved (see page 16). When grown in pots these plants prefer a John Innes Compost No. 2 mixed with one third of sharp sand.

Planting Planting out in the garden is normally done in late spring when the fear of frosts has passed, using plants raised from seed the previous summer. Echium have long thin tap roots and they dislike transplanting, so it is essential that they are planted out into their final positions as young plants with the least possible root disturbance. Plants must be watered in well and may need some simple staking in exposed coastal areas until they are established.

AFTERCARE

Feeding Echium grown in pots appreciate a liquid feed with a high-potash fertilizer applied once a month during the growing season. Plants in the garden require only a light dressing of fertilizer at planting time.

Pruning After flowering plants normally die, but occasionally a second rosette is produced and when this happens the flowered stem can be cut back as it withers to encourage the new rosette. Other than this no pruning is required.

Winter Protection In cold districts echium will need winter protection, as their tap roots mean they cannot be dug up and brought inside. Wrap some strips of horticultural fleece around the stem and put a thick mulch of bracken around the plant to prevent the roots from freezing. You should then place a polythene sheet of 1m (3ft) in diameter over this, so that it covers the surrounding soil. It should be higher in the centre and fall away from the plant to deflect the winter wet away from the roots. The crown should also be wrapped up in fleece; a simple sack method supported by canes is best as it can be removed in mild weather to allow the plant some air and prevent fungal diseases.

Pests & Diseases Echium are usually trouble free, although aphids can attack plants when they are grown under glass.

PROPAGATION

Echium are normally raised from seed which germinates very freely. It should be sown in an open gritty compost comprised of half coir and half sharp grit. Seeds that have fallen from old plants will germinate in the border during warm moist spells. These can be lifted and potted when they are 5cm (2in) high; take care not to damage the roots. *E. pininana* is not propagated by cuttings, but some of the more shrubby species can be, by taking semi-ripe cuttings of lateral shoots in summer.

OTHER VARIETIES

E. wildpretii H & S: 1.5 x 1m (5 x 3ft). Its leaves are covered in silver hairs which give the whole plant a silver sheen. The flower spike containing hundreds of small red flowers is only produced after the third or fourth year. An interesting and beautiful species, it will tolerate cold, but not winter wet. A simple cloche should keep it dry enough. *E. candicans* H & S: 1.5 x 1.25m (5 x 4ft). A shrubby species from Madeira, it can have three or more spikes flowering at one time. The leaves are silvery-green and the flowers dark blue streaked with white.

Salvia guaranitica

Salvia are a huge group of plants with 900 or more species and countless cultivars. They include common plants like the herb sage, *S. officinalis*, and the stunning biennial *S. sclarea*. They grow around the world from the Mediterranean and the grassy plains of Central Asia to the dry scrublands of California. *Salvia guaranitica* is one of a group of half-hardy species originating from Central and South America which are increasing in popularity with a stunning range of flower colours and plant forms to choose from.

Many are tender and have to be brought inside during winter, but some will survive outside for many years in the right situation. *S. guaranitica* typifies the conditions that many other species thrive in, tolerating temperatures as low as -10°C (14°F).

A superb plant, with strong and erect growth, it can reach 1.5m (5ft) in one season and spread to 60-100cm (2-3ft). Its leaves are rough and dark green, forming the perfect foil for the long (up to 5cm [2in]), tubular, dark blue flowers which appear in mid summer until the first frosts (see page 20). *S. guaranitica* is the perfect companion to other warmth-seeking perennials, like penstemon, artemisia and diascia.

CULTIVATION

Site Selection Salvia require shelter from strong and cold winds, a well-drained soil and full sun. They thrive when planted in a south- or south-west-facing aspect. In cold areas they will need the shelter afforded by a warm wall or they may have to be lifted and brought into a frost-free greenhouse or conservatory for the winter, but in most gardens they can be grown in the open border. In mild or coastal gardens they can still be flowering on Christmas Day.

Soil Half-hardy salvia prefer a medium-fertile, well-drained soil which will not dry out in summer. They will grow in heavy soils, but can rot during winter, so if your soil tends towards this type you should improve it (see page 16). Free-draining sandy soils are often too dry during summer, resulting in constant wilting and reduced plant growth. Avoid adding rich organic matter as this promotes too much soft plant growth which is prone to cold damage. Plants grown in containers should be potted into a soil-based compost, such as John Innes No. 2.

Planting This usually takes place in the spring after the threat of frosts has passed. Young plants that have been grown under glass are fragile and prone to wind damage, so they should be tied to a short cane until they have had time to establish. If they do collapse, they will nearly always reshoot from the base and this growth will be stronger and better able to withstand damage, although *S. guaranitica* is one of the more wind-resistant species. Plants should be planted to the same depth as they were in their pots and watered in well. On soils with low fertility the addition of an organic fertilizer in spring helps to promote healthy strong growth.

AFTERCARE

Feeding Salvia require little feeding when grown outside in the garden. Plants grown in containers will need feeding fortnightly through the growing season with a liquid fertilizer high in potash.

Pruning During the growing season, salvia require little pruning except for the removal of the occasional damaged branch. At the end of the year stems should be cut down to 15cm (6in). These can be cut down further in spring to remove winter-damaged tissue and to prune to the level of emerging new shoots.

Winter Protection Plants left outside should be given a heavy mulch of chopped bracken or straw, held down with pea netting. Don't use coir, compost or manures as they absorb too much water and cause the plants to rot. Often salvia that have been properly protected during their first couple of winters will establish themselves sufficiently not to need such a heavy mulch in future years, emerging in late spring even after hard winters.

Pests & Diseases Few pests and diseases affect plants outside, but slugs and snails can be a problem in spring when the new growth is emerging. Whitefly are the biggest problem for plants grown under glass and they can spread quickly.

PROPAGATION

Salvia are very easily propagated from softwood cuttings in summer or semi-ripe cuttings in autumn. Both these methods produce large numbers of plants quickly and provide a supply of young plants to replace ones outside that are killed off during winter.

OTHER VARIETIES

S. uliginosa H & S: 2.5 x 0.5m (8 x 1½ft). The flower spikes are thin, graceful and topped with sky-blue flowers in an arrow-shaped head. *S. involucrata* 'Mrs Pope' H & S: 1.5 x 1.2m (5 x 4ft). This has stout stems and matt green, hairy leaves. It produces a terminal spike up to 30cm (12in) with large tubular 3-cm- (1¼-in)-long deep cerise-red flowers that appear in summer and last till autumn.

Tropaeolum speciosum
(FLAME CREEPER)

Often seen growing up yew hedges in gardens on the west coast of Scotland (hence one of its other common names, the Scottish flame flower), this delightful herbaceous self-clinging climber provides an abundance of vivid pillar-box red flowers from the middle of summer right through to early autumn (see page 40). It is a real moisture-lover and although hedges provide an ideal background for it, don't plant it next to a conifer hedge, such as *Leylandii* or Lawson cypress, as they take all the moisture from the ground.

It will grow as high as 3m (10ft) and spread to 1.5m (5ft), but dies back to its rootstock during the winter months and then sends out new shoots in spring. And it can tolerate temperatures as low as -10°C (14°F). *T. speciosum* can take a while to establish, but once it is happy in its position it can be almost weed-like and will grow very freely.

CULTIVATION

Site Selection Its ideal home would be against a west- or southwest-facing wall or fence where it should receive the right amount of warmth and moisture. But if it is well-protected from winds by fences or surrounding walls, it can survive a north-facing aspect and, for example, might do well in an urban courtyard garden. Tropaeolum succumb very easily in conditions that are too dry, so a south-facing site would be too much for it.

Soil Tropaeolum prefer a moisture-retentive, but free-draining organic soil, especially during the

A vigorous climber, the attractive Tropaeolum speciosum *is set off to perfection by the dark green leaves of its host plant.*

~

fertilizer. When planting it against a hedge, tie it in to the parent plant, or else provide it with a cane or some trellis for it to twine round.

AFTERCARE

Feeding Generally, tropaeolum don't need a lot of feeding. You might want to give them the odd dressing of fertilizer in the spring if your soil is particularly weak, or if it is a free-draining sandy type. However, container-grown plants will benefit during the growing season from a regular feed of a weak solution of liquid fertilizer.

Pruning In some ways this can present a problem since tropaeolum tend to twine

summer months, so heavy or sandy soils will need improving (see page 16). They like neutral or slightly acidic conditions, so gardeners in chalky or limestone areas might prefer to grow them in containers or in a raised bed.

Planting Plants should be put out in spring once the fear of frosts has passed and the ground is starting to warm up. If you lift the plant and pot it up in a cool greenhouse during the winter, you may find that it will start growing very early on and spread all over the place even though it hasn't received any water, but this is not a problem. When planting it outside, put it in its final position and water it in. If you have prepared the soil as above, the tropaeolum shouldn't need any additional

around themselves as well as around their support. But really they don't need any attention until the end of the growing season when they are cut down to ground level and tidied up. If you do prune during the season, always cut to a lateral shoot or bud. You may find this necessary if the tropaeolum is smothering a host plant, and it can be trimmed down by about a third. It should recover quickly.

Winter Protection *T. speciosum* is quite hardy in the right situation, but if it is in an exposed position I suggest giving it an organic mulch of chopped bracken or leaf mould and covering this with a small sheet of polythene to deflect the winter rains.

Pests & Diseases Usually tropaeolum are disease-free, though there is a virus which can cause the leaves to yellow and develop brown spots. At its very worst it can check the plant's growth so much that it dies. Young plants can be prone to attacks from aphids in spring and plants which have been overwintered in the greenhouse can suffer from attacks of whitefly, as can plants grown in containers outside. (See Pests & Diseases page 19.)

PROPAGATION

Tropaeolum are usually propagated either by division or by seed. If propagating by division, dig the tubers up during the dormant season, break off the new tubers and pot them up. Seed sown in the late winter or early spring will germinate quite quickly at a temperature of 13-16°C (55-60°F). If, however, you are feeling green-fingered, you might want to try taking some semi-ripe cuttings of short laterals in the summertime when the new season's growth is just beginning to harden off. Make sure you choose laterals that are young and strong – most are about 15cm (6in) long – and avoid any that are long and wiry. Pot them up in a free-draining compost mix and put a polythene bag over the top. Keep the cuttings in a well-lit position out of direct sunlight. They may take some time to root and can be helped by some hormone rooting powder.

OTHER VARIETIES

T. tuberosum H & S: 3 x 1.5m (10 x 5ft). It has orange-red flowers with deep orange tips and rather glaucous grey-green leaves. It is important to make sure the soil's drainage is adequate before planting this variety. *T. tuberosum*, 'Ken Aslet' H & S: 3 x 1.5m (10 x 5ft). This cultivar is quite similar to the species, but its flowers are mainly orange.

MORE TENDER PLANTS TO TRY

~

Abutilon megapotamicum H & S: 2 x 1.5m (6 x 5ft). An attractive, evergreen, small, Brazilian shrub with thin wiry stems and deep olive-green leaves which is hardy down to 10°C (14°F). It produces a profusion of small, lantern-like yellow and red flowers from early summer to autumn.

Acacia dealbata (Silver Wattle or Mimosa) H & S: 7 x 3m (20 x 10ft). This Australian mimosa makes a beautiful evergreen wall shrub, but in mild areas it can be planted out in the sheltered border where it can reach tree-like porportions. Its silver-green foliage is delicate, and it only tolerates frosts (down to about -5°C (23°F) for a short period. Flower buds appear in autumn and clouds of small golden-yellow blossoms cover the shrub in late winter. It prefers a well-drained but moisture-retentive soil.

Brugmansia sanguinea syn. *Datura sanguinea* (Red Angel's Trumpet) H & S: 1.5 x 1m (5 x 3ft). A small, semi-evergreen shrub, it has dark green foliage and fat succulent stems. Its long trumpet-like yellow flowers are tipped with red and are produced over a long period in summer. Hardy down to -2°C (29°F), it is beau-tifully scented, but all parts of the plant are poisonous.

Canna x *generalis* H & S: 2 x 1m (6 x 3ft). A beautiful rhizomatous perennial that originates from the sub-tropics. It has oval, lanceolate dark green and brown leaves. These really set off the numerous tubular-shaped orange-yellow flowers that are produced in summer. Hardy down to -5°C (23°F), it will tolerate some shade as long as it spends the majority of the day in full sun and it likes a moisture-retentive soil. It is also good for growing in containers.

Hedychium gardnerianum (Kahili Ginger) H & S: 2 x 1m (6 x 3ft). An herbaceous perennial with long, mid-green leaves and bright yellow and orange, scented flowers that appear on a tall spike in late summer and autumn. It is hardy down to -5°C (23°F).

Hardy Sun-loving Plants

~

If you want a garden that really looks good, it has to contain at least one or two hardy sun-loving plants. They provide a striking range of foliage in all shapes and sizes and masses of glorious colour during the summer when your garden should be looking its best. As you might expect, all the plants mentioned here thrive in full sun and like the tender plants they come from similar parts of the world, such as Australia, South Africa and the Mediterranean, as well as the warmer areas of North America like California.

Depending on where you live, hardy sun-loving plants are usually more tolerant of bad weather than tender ones, but in cold areas they may need some winter protection. They don't like cold north and easterly winds, but they will tolerate fairly strong westerly winds and maritime conditions, so species such as cordyline and callistemon make excellent choices for coastal gardens.

SITE SELECTION

Hardy sun-loving plants share a preference for south-, west- or southwest-facing walls with their cousins, the tender plants, particularly when it comes to colder areas. But while tender plants may only survive in these most sheltered locations, hardy sun-loving plants can grow quite happily in the open border in milder situations. A mixture of shrubs in the surrounding area usually provides them with enough protection. If you are in any doubt, though, opt for the safety of a wall where they can be planted as close to the base as possible – about 15-30cm (6-12in) – and enjoy similar benefits as the tender plants, receiving the reflected heat that ensures good growth and flowering and sufficient shelter from the cold winter winds.

SOIL

Hardy sun-loving plants appreciate a well-drained, but moisture-retentive soil. It should never become waterlogged, however, as this can quickly lead to suffocation and death of the roots. These plants will be happy enough in a wide range of garden soils, as long as they are well drained. But should your soil be particularly heavy or have been neglected for some time and therefore in poor condition, you must improve it. To find out more about how to improve your soil see the first chapter, page 16.

PLANTING

Like the tender plants, hardy sun-loving plants are usually planted out in the late spring, once the threat of frost has passed and the soil has begun to warm up. If necessary, though, you can continue planting through the summer until early autumn.

If you do plant during the summer, be careful that you don't allow the plants to dry out. A young plant can soon stop growing if it doesn't receive enough water on a hot summer's day. This leads to poor plant establishment and eventually death. So water the plant in well and add a mulch to conserve the soil's moisture. Once the plant is established it will rarely need a mulch or summer watering.

Before planting, prepare the soil thoroughly (see page 22). A large shrub like *Fremontodendron californicum* might be in your garden for the next 20 years, so it's worth spending the time cultivating the soil in the planting area. Add some organic matter and fork it into the base of the planting hole. Make sure that the soil you use for backfilling also has some organic matter added to it and that it is spread in and around the roots of the plant. Gently firm the soil in using the ball of your foot, not the heel, and apply a little pressure. For bulbs such as agapanthus and nerine, it is probably worth adding some sharp gravel to the soil that you are using to backfill the planting hole, even if your soil is well drained, because they need good drainage during winter.

The final thing to consider is whether the plant needs a stake or cane support, which young shrubs most certainly will do until they have settled in.

WINTER PROTECTION

Although the plants in this chapter are hardy, they may need some simple winter protection until they are established. Young plants can sometimes suffer during winter when strong winds create a low wind-chill factor. If plants are likely to succumb to the ravages of winds, it may be worthwhile erecting a simple netting screen around them to reduce the wind speed and the effects of the wind chill.

Phygelius aequalis
'Yellow Trumpet'
(CAPE FUSCHIA)

One of a stunning range of evergreen shrubs which in their natural climate can reach a height of 3m (10ft), but in colder climates usually behave as semi-herbaceous plants with the cold winters cutting them down. However, that does not mean that phygelius cannot tolerate frost. Usually, they will survive temperatures of as little as 5°C (23°F) and I have known *Phygelius aequalis* 'Yellow Trumpet' cope with a winter of -10°C (14°F).

In the right conditions this is a sturdy plant, forming a dense shrub which throws up shoots that can grow up to 30cm (12in) in one year. It will reach a height of 1.5m (5ft) and a spread of 1.25m (4ft) and produces terminal spikes of pendulous tubular-shaped flowers which are creamy yellow and a slightly deeper yellow inside and which can be up to 7.5cm (3in) long (see page 44). These appear from early to mid summer while some of the other species, such as *P. capensis,* will flower for longer.

P. aequalis 'Yellow Trumpet' looks good as part of a sub-tropical planting scheme and goes well with such plants as *Canna* x *generalis* (see page 41) and some of the cordyline (see page 53).

CULTIVATION

Site Selection Phygelius like a warm, sunny location, so a west- or southwest-facing aspect is ideal. But they also need a moist, well-drained soil during the summer. And they like to be protected from cold winds which can do a lot of damage.

Soil These plants hate having their roots in a cold heavy soil which can result in winter losses. If your soil is like this, try to raise the bed to improve the drainage or plant the phygelius in a terraced bed. Equally, thin soils can produce scrappy plants, since phygelius like an adequate supply of nutrients.

Planting Normally phygelius should be planted in spring, once the fear of frosts has passed, but they can be planted right through the summer and should settle in quickly and produce new growth easily. Instead of planting them in the middle of the border where they will form a clump, you can position them at the base of a wall and train them on wires to create an attractive background. If you do this, you will prevent the plant from sprawling around, which can happen if they are left to their own devices, but wall-trained plants will need more pruning. With phygelius it is important to water the new plants in well to help them settle in.

AFTERCARE

Feeding Container-grown phygelius will need a weekly feed of a general fertilizer during the growing season (usually May-September) to keep them in peak condition. Phygelius grown in a bed shouldn't need feeding unless they show signs of being slightly chlorotic. If they are, they should respond quickly to a balanced liquid fertilizer.

Pruning The important thing to do is to deadhead flowering stems by cutting them back by about half their length to where the stronger leaves are. These stems should then branch out and form new stout flowering stems later on in the season. At the end of the year plants can be tidied up with a general prune to keep them in shape and to take off the dead flower heads. Semi-herbaceous ones, like *P. capensis,* will need pruning again in the spring when you should remove the old stems from the previous year, allowing new stems, which should just be coming through, to grow on strongly.

Winter Protection In cold districts phygelius will benefit from a covering of horticultural fleece in frosty conditions.

Pests & Diseases Relatively trouble-free, but may suffer from attacks of aphids in spring.

PROPAGATION

It is very easy to grow phygelius from softwood or semi-ripe cuttings, with the former being taken in high summer and the latter in late summer or early autumn. Use any good cutting compost, or make your own with half measures of vermiculite and either peat substitute or chopped bark. Cuttings should be about 10cm (4in) long and taken at a leaf joint with the bottom pair of leaves removed. They should root within a month. Alternatively, you can grow phygelius from seed, which should be collected in late summer. Either keep the seed and sow it in early spring under glass at a temperature of 15-18°C (60-65°F), or sow it in a heated greenhouse in the autumn and leave the plants in their seed pots through the winter. Pot them up in spring

Stone walls are very useful for reflecting the sun's warmth on to surrounding plants like the yellow-flowered Phygelius aequalis 'Yellow Trumpet'.

and let them grow on for a while before putting them out in their final location.

OTHER VARIETIES

P. aequalis H & S: 1.5 x 1.25m (5 x 4ft). This has beautiful, dusky pink flowers with orange-coloured mouths and yellow throats and glossy, dark green leaves. *P. capensis* H & S: 1.25 x 1m (4 x 3ft). Its flowers are bright red with a deep yellow throat. *P.* 'Moonraker' H & S: 2 x 1.25m (6 x 4ft). Another cultivar which is a cross between *P. aequalis* 'Yellow Trumpet' and *P.* x *rectus* 'Winchester Fanfare'. It has lanceolate, tooth-edged leaves and narrow, pale yellow flowers.

Nerine bowdenii

Originally from South Africa, this unusual bulbous plant provides a lot of interest throughout the summer and autumn. First producing soft, fleshy, bright green leaves which die off during the summer, *Nerine bowdenii* then throws up tall flower spikes that can reach 60cm (2ft) and which are completely bare. But at their tops they have a profusion of brilliant cerise-pink, trumpet-shaped flowers and clumps of these can make a lovely feature in any garden (see right). They look good when partnered by tender perennials such as *Salvia patens* or argyranthemum or osteospermum because they will come up through these plants and flower just above them when the perennials are still flowering in early autumn.

A fairly hardy plant, *N. bowdenii* can tolerate temperatures down to approximately -15°C (5°F), although only for a short time and if this sort of temperature were combined with very wet conditions then it is likely that the nerine could die. For these reasons, you often find nerine planted up against the wall of a house or greenhouse where overhanging roofs can provide some shelter.

CULTIVATION

Site Selection Nerine really prefer a south- or southwest-facing aspect which should offer some protection from rain. As long as it is warm and has good light, they will thrive in a situation where many other plants would dry and wither. It is most important that the sunlight reaches the base since too much shade from adjacent plants can reduce the initiation of the following year's flower buds.

Soil If you do plant them out in a border, then it is essential that the soil is free-draining, otherwise the

The beautiful Nerine bowdenii *flourishes in full sun and warmth at the front of the border. Its impressive pink flower heads contrast well with the deep blue of the* Salvia patens *behind.*

~

plant will rot in the winter months. If your garden soil is generally heavy, you can plant the nerine in a pot or a raised bed. The other alternative is to replace the soil in the growing area with a good, well-draining mixture. In fact it is wise, when planting, to put a layer of grit in the base of the planting hole which the bulb can sit on. Its roots will then grow through the grit into the soil below. It isn't necessary to have a very rich soil since these plants can tolerate fairly poor soils.

Planting Nerine can be bought in their dormant stage during the late summer and they should be planted straight away. It is important not to plant the bulb completely in the ground as one would with a daffodil or tulip. Nerine naturally have their bulb necks near the surface and form dense clumps, and if you do plant the bulb too deep it may well rot.

During the latter part of the winter and early spring plants can be moved while they are in active growth, provided they are watered in well. Large clumps can be dug up and divided and put in their new positions where they should settle in quite quickly. It is best to do this before the flower stalks appear, so the other time for this job is when the plant is dormant during the summer.

AFTERCARE

Feeding Nerine require very little feeding. If you are growing them in a pot, then a high-potash feed is a good idea at the height of the season. This should cease once the foliage starts to dry off in high summer.

Pruning There is not much to do in the way of pruning. Dead leaves can be pulled off from mid to late summer and dead flower spikes should be removed when they have withered away and died.

Winter Protection This is important, particularly in cold areas, because the necks of the bulbs must be protected from long periods of frost. Ideally, you should use a thick mulch of some sort of dry material such as straw or bracken, or you can cover the crowns in a double layer of horticultural fleece.

Pests & Diseases Generally, nerine are free from pests and diseases, but in heavy wet soils they can be prone to rot. If, when lifting plants, you discover any rot, cut out the affected area, back to healthy tissue, and dust the cut with sulphur powder before putting the bulbs in their new position.

PROPAGATION

Division is the main way of propagating nerine. Clumps can be dug up and, as long as they have a leading shoot and some roots developing at the base, new bulbs can be cut off and planted to form more clumps. It is also possible to propagate by seed which should be sown fresh, either in the autumn or the following spring, in a general seed compost and kept at a temperature of about 20°C (68°F). The seed should germinate quickly and young plants are normally potted up in groups of two or three to form established clumps.

OTHER VARIETIES

N. bowdenii 'Alba' H & S: 60 x 40cm (48 x 16in). A stunning variety with white flowers that have just a blush of pink. *N. sarniensis* (Guernsey Lily) H & S: 45 x 30cm (18 x 12in). Produces bright red or pink flowers in groups of ten to twenty on each spike.

Eccremocarpus scaber aurantiacus
(CHILEAN GLORY FLOWER, GLORY VINE)

I have known this delightful evergreen climber to be still flowering on Christmas Day, if the autumn has been mild. But generally *Eccremocarpus scaber aurantiacus* produces its beautiful pendulous pale orange flowers all the way through summer into early autumn (see page 17). It is reasonably hardy and should tolerate temperatures down to about -5°C (23°F) or -10°C (14°F), if it is grown in a sheltered location.

Originating from Chile, as their common name suggests, eccremocarpus are seen to their best advantage when mixed with other climbers, particularly ivies, or growing through shrubs, since their stems can look untidy.

CULTIVATION

Site Selection If you are planting eccremocarpus against a wall, a west-, southwest- or south-facing location is best. But, they do need a position where they will receive direct sunlight for at least half the day. They also hate wind, so avoid east-facing sites and make sure they have some shelter.

Soil Eccremocarpus like a sandy, well-drained soil which is neutral to slightly acidic. So clay soils need to be improved to give better drainage and aeration, or the soil around the planting area should be removed and replaced with a more appropriate mixture.

Planting Plants can be put in once the fear of frosts has passed in spring and indeed all through the summer. Make sure that the soil is thoroughly prepared and that it is well drained and not waterlogged. Add a little organic fertilizer to the hole and plant the eccremocarpus to the same depth as it was in its pot and water it in well. Young plants should be tied into their climbing supports to prevent them from wind damage.

AFTERCARE

Feeding Eccremocarpus are undemanding plants as long as the soil around them is fairly fertile, but a base dressing hoed in around the plants in late spring should provide enough nutrients for the whole season. If the soil is weak, some additional organic matter can help. And if the eccremocarpus are in a container, a helping of a slow-release fertilizer should keep them happy for the season. Alternatively, you could feed them with a liquid manure from spring through to the end of summer.

Pruning These plants can be a bit ungainly and they can get very large. In addition, because of their tendrils which cling on to the host plant or support, pruning can be rather difficult. It is probably best to keep the plant pruned throughout the growing season to the required size and shape, but usually pruning is done at the end of winter when the plants can be deadwooded and cut back to about 1-1.25m (3-4ft) to shoots which are appearing lower down. These shoots will grow very quickly and soon provide the new branch structure for the next lot of flowers.

Winter Protection In cold districts the top growth may be killed during the winter months, but eccremocarpus often regenerate from just below ground level and are rarely killed, providing they are in the correct location. A heavy mulch of dry leaf material or bracken can help to insulate the plant.

Pests & Diseases Generally eccremocarpus are free of any pests and diseases, but occasionally young shoots may suffer an attack of aphids in the spring.

PROPAGATION

This is normally done by seed and plants produce masses of black winged seeds. These should be sown thinly in the spring on a well-drained seed compost, covered very lightly and kept at a temperature of about 13-16°C (55-60°F). Germination is very easy and usually takes place within four to six weeks. It is interesting to note that plants raised from seed can often flower in their first year.

You can also take cuttings in early summer and these should be taken at a leaf bud, or as soft wood cuttings, and kept at a reasonably cool temperature, 20°C (68°F), in a propagation case or in a pot with a polythene bag over the top as soft growth can wilt quite quickly if it is too hot.

OTHER VARIETIES

E. scaber 'Warius' H & S: 3 x 2.1m (10 x 7ft). Very attractive with golden-yellow flowers that are semi-translucent. *E. scaber* 'Carmineus' H & S: 3 x 2.1m (10 x 7ft). A cultivar with deep red flowers.

Ceanothus thyrsiflorus var. *repens*

(CALIFORNIAN LILAC)

Originating from the west of America (hence its common name) and Mexico, this beautiful shrub is renowned for the mass of bright blue flowers which appear every summer (see opposite). There are numerous species and hybrid varieties in cultivation, most of which are evergreen, though a few are deciduous. They love sunny conditions and are ideal for coastal districts since they can tolerate strong salt-laden winds. Ceanothus flourish against sunny walls and with other plants originating from California such as *Fremontodendron californicum* (see page 58). But they will also do well with Australian plants such as eucalyptus and callistemon (see page 55) which all thrive in similar conditions.

C thyrsiflorus var. *repens* is quite compact in habit, reaching a height of 1.25m (4ft) and a spread of 2.5m (8ft). With its shiny, dark olive green leaves and bright blue flowers it looks very attractive and is hardier than other ceanothus tolerating temperatures as low as -15°C (5°F).

CULTIVATION

Site Selection Ceanothus do best against a south- or southwest-facing wall where they can get plenty of warmth and sun. In mild conditions they will do well in an open border. *C. thyrsiflorus* var. *repens* tolerates partial shade, but prefers the sun. It doesn't like being exposed to cold winter winds.

Soil These plants need a good, moist, fertile soil which must also be well-drained, since heavy, wet soil can lead to rotting roots during winter. If the summer is particularly dry, though, ceanothus can cope with a little drought in free-draining soils.

Planting This is normally done in spring when young plants can be put in their final positions. Container-grown plants can be potted up any time during late spring, summer or early autumn when the soil is still warm. Plants should be planted at the same depth as they were in their pots and staked until they are fully established. Alternatively, if you are placing the ceanothus against a wall or a fence, they can be tied in to wires, which is important if you are training the plants into a fan shape.

AFTERCARE

Feeding If the soil is reasonably fertile, ceanothus will require very little feeding. If you do have to feed them, then a high-potash fertilizer is best. A general fertilizer can be applied in spring to give plants a boost in the coming months. Plants in containers may need a weekly liquid feed during the growing season, from mid spring until the end of the summer, to keep them healthy.

Pruning As ceanothus usually flower on last season's wood, they need a light pruning just after flowering. However, they may need pruning more severely to cut out any growth that has been killed during a hard winter. Often, after a hard winter, plants will regenerate and begin to shoot from near ground level. Dead wood should be pruned back to living tissue. Too-frequent pruning or clipping can shorten the life of the plant. The deciduous species tend to flower in late summer and early autumn and should be pruned in the spring when growth resumes. In this case, the previous season's growth is cut back to about two pairs of buds.

Winter Protection Only in the coldest areas will ceanothus need some winter protection. However, young plants need something like a piece of horticultural fleece draped over to protect them in their first year. This can be held in place by a couple of canes. It can then be taken off during milder spells to allow the plant the light and air that it needs.

Pests & Diseases Young, tender growth is sometimes affected by aphids in spring, but usually ceanothus tend to be pest and disease free. Old, established plants can die suddenly in summer and you should remember that ceanothus are best grown as young plants and those that are about 15 years old or more may need replacing as they often flower heavily and then die the following year.

PROPAGATION

Ceanothus can be propagated by seeds which need to be stratified for a minimum of 30 days and ideally should have longer – up to 90 days. This can be done in moist sand or a proprietary seed compost either in autumn, when they should be left in a cold frame so they can spend some time at a temperature of about 1-5°C (34-41°F), and should

also be kept moist, or in spring when they should go into the fridge. If you do put them in the fridge, make sure that the compost doesn't dry out. After stratification, the seeds should be placed in a temperature of 21°C (70°F) to germinate.

Alternatively, ceanothus can be propagated by softwood or semi-ripe nodal cuttings which should be taken either in summer or early autumn. Dip the ends of the cuttings in a hormone rooting powder and put them into some free-draining cutting compost.

Ceanothus thyrsiflorus *var.* repens' *habit makes it ideal for planting at the front of a sunny border.*

~

OTHER VARIETIES

C. arboreus 'Trewithen Blue' H & S: 4 x 4m (12 x 12ft). It is an evergreen and has dark green leaves. In late spring it is covered with large bunches of powder blue flowers. *C. x pallidus* 'Marie Simon' H & S: 2.5 x 2.5m (8 x 8ft). A deciduous variety with unusual young red stems, rather like dogwood and light pink flowers. *C. x dileanus* 'Gloire de Versailles' H & S: 3 x 2.5m (10 x 8ft). Has bright green leaves and pale blue flowers that appear in late spring and early summer.

Agapanthus comptonii

The range of agapanthus is astounding and any one of this family of plants can provide a delightful focus in the garden, either towering over low-growing sun-loving plants like *Lobelia laxiflora, L. siphilitica* or *L. tupa,* or complemented by other summer-flowering bulbs such as crocosmia, nerine (see page 45), acidanthera or kniphofia. They are elegant and graceful and make a beautiful addition to flower arrangements.

A comptonii, which I grow, produces large roundels of sky blue flowers that have paler blue streaks down their sides (see page 20).

Although the majority of agapanthus are hardy, the evergreen *A. comptonii* is less so, only coping with a temperature of about -5°C (23°F). It will reach a height of just over 1m (3½ft) and plants will spread to 60cm (2ft).

CULTIVATION

Site Selection Since agapanthus originate from South Africa, they must have sun in order to grow successfully. In colder climates they do best in a south- or south-west-facing position, usually up against a wall to receive some of the protection that that can afford them. If planted in warmer areas in an open border, they like to be free of shade.

Soil Ideally, these beautiful plants prefer a well-drained, quite fertile soil which will retain moisture in the summer months, but which will not become waterlogged. One of the best ways to grow them in cooler areas is to put them in a container which can then be brought indoors during the winter months. And they can stay in their final size container for several years. If your soil is rather weak or sandy, it is worth adding some organic matter to increase its fertility. Heavy soils will need lots of grit or the addition of an improver, such as vermiculite – anything to open them up.

Planting This is usually done in late spring when growth has commenced and it is possible to buy young plants which can be put out in their final positions. Do make sure that the soil is thoroughly prepared and, if possible, put some grit in the base of the planting hole for each bulb to stand on. This will help to prevent them from rotting. The necks of the bulbs should be quite near the surface and just showing. Once in their final positions, bulbs should remain there for several years. Established clumps can be dug up during the spring just before flowering commences, which is usually in summer through to autumn, and divided. Providing the divided plants are watered in well, they should soon settle down and produce more growth as the season continues.

AFTERCARE

Feeding Agapanthus do need some feeding, particularly when they are grown in pots or containers. A general liquid feed or one high in potash applied from early summer until the flower heads have formed is a good idea. After that it should be withheld, otherwise too much soft growth will be promoted, making the plants prone to winter rot. During the spring, established clumps should be given a sprinkling of bonemeal hoed into the surrounding soil.

Pruning These plants need very little pruning. If seed is not required, the dead flower stalks should be cut down to the first or second basal leaf. And in spring the dead leaves should be tidied up.

Winter Protection In cold areas where agapanthus are being grown outside it is a good idea to protect the plants with an insulating mulch, such as chopped bracken, and some horticultural fleece. Avoid using peat, wood shavings, compost or coir which can retain too much moisture.

Container-grown plants can be moved indoors into a frost-free greenhouse, conservatory or shed to overwinter.

Pests & Diseases The main pest problem is slugs and snails which eat the young foliage and shred the more mature foliage. This is particularly a problem in areas which are quite damp and in the spring when new growth is emerging.

PROPAGATION

It is not difficult to propagate agapanthus. Large established crowns or overcrowded crowns can be lifted and divided, usually by inserting two forks back to back and splitting them into more manageable sizes. These are then potted up or replanted and watered in. Offsets can also be cut off established crowns as long as there is a well-formed bulb with a new shoot developing. These should soon make sizeable clumps.

Alternatively, agapanthus can be raised from seed. It germinates very easily whether it is sown fresh or in the spring. The only disadvantage is that seed-grown plants can take as long as two to three years before first flowering. Sow the seed on a well-drained seed compost, cover lightly and keep at a temperature of about 21°C (70°F).

OTHER VARIETIES

A. africanus (African Lily, Blue African Lily or Lily of the Nile) H & S: 60 x 60cm (2 x 2ft). An evergreen species with violet-blue flowers of about 2.5-5cm (1-2in) long. There is also a white form. *A. campanulatus.* H & S: 1 x 1m (3 x 3ft). This has lighter blue flowers and again there is a white variety.

Asphodeline lutea

(KING'S SPEAR, YELLOW ASPHODELINE)

Growing to a height of about 1 x 1.25m (3-4ft) and with a spread of 40cm (16in), this native of southern Europe makes a beautiful addition to the herbaceous border or it can be naturalized on a rocky bank. With its long thin leaves that have a blue-grey sheen, *Asphodeline lutea* looks really spectacular (see page 53). By habit it forms a clump and in late spring or early summer tall flower spikes appear which produce star-shaped, bright sunshine-yellow flowers that bloom in succession throughout the season (which is quite long for this plant). The flowers, which have a lovely fragrance,

open early in the morning and fade by evening. And when the flowering period is over the asphodeline produces round, marble-sized seed pods which look quite striking. It looks good with salvia (see page 38) and *Convolvulus cneorum* (see page 59).

It is quite hardy, tolerating temperatures of as low as -15°C (5°F).

CULTIVATION

Site Selection Asphodeline prefer a sunny position but will thrive in most situations as long as they get direct sun for at least half the day. They won't tolerate too much shade.

Soil A well-drained, moisture-retentive soil is best, but they are not happy in extremes of either waterlogged soil or in drought conditions. The soil should also be moderately fertile. Asphodeline can tolerate heavy soils as long as they don't get waterlogged during the winter. If the soil is thin and sandy, then it should be improved to help retain some moisture during the summer. Contrarily, asphodeline dislike soil that is too rich. This can promote too much foliage which suffers during the winter and can result in the plant dying.

Planting This normally takes place in spring, but potted plants can be put out any time during the growing season. They even do well when planted in autumn, or at least before the soil gets too cold. The plants should be planted at the same depth as they were in the pot and watered in well. To help young plants establish a healthy clump, it is a good idea to cut off the first flower spike so that strong basal roots are produced. The plants can then start flowering in their second year. Mulching can be useful on thin, dry soils.

AFTERCARE

Feeding Asphodeline aren't very demanding plants, but they do appreciate a dressing of general fertilizer in late spring to give them some nourishment later in the growing season.

Pruning Although these plants are perennials, they aren't totally herbaceous and the rosettes of leaves should never be cut right down to ground level. This is important since asphodeline should always keep some foliage above the ground during winter. Dead flower spikes can be cut off if seed production is not needed. Otherwise, collect the seed pods just before they begin to crack open and then the flower spikes can be cut down to the fresh leaves near the base.

Winter Protection Only in the coldest localities do asphodeline need some protection during the winter. Siting them near a building can help to give them protection if the area is very very cold.

Pests & Diseases Generally trouble-free, young foliage may attract black fly in spring. The main predators are slugs and snails which congregate under the leaves during winter and feed on new shoots and flower spikes. They can be picked off.

PROPAGATION

Plants can be divided towards the end of the winter and in early spring, but it is important to ensure that the offsets have sufficient roots so that they establish successfully and it is a good idea to divide older plants into quite large segments. If they are too small, they can take a long time to get going.

Seed can be sown either in the autumn or early spring and should be kept quite cool at about 15-18°C (60-65°F). Germination, especially from seed sown in the autumn, takes place quite quickly. Prick out seedlings two to a pot and let them grow on for another year. These should be protected from the worst of the winter weather to make sure they are not killed off by the cold and from slugs and snails.

OTHER VARIETIES

A. lutea 'Flore Plena' H & S: 120 x 40cm (48 x 16in). Has long-lasting, golden yellow, double flowers. *A. liburnica* H & S: 60 x 30cm (2 x 1ft). Also a perennial which produces yellow flowers that are striped with green. A native of south-eastern Europe, it is very handsome.

~

Full sunshine is vital for the vigorous growth of bottle brushes such as the stunning yellow-flowered Callistemon pallidus *(page 55), and the spiky-leaved* Cordyline australis *(opposite) which both originate from the Antipodes.*

The white spikes of Eremurus stenophyllus
(page 56) and the yellow Asphodeline lutea *(page 51)*
contrast well with the little flowers of
Vestia foetida *(page 25), behind them.*

~

Cordyline australis

(NEW ZEALAND CABBAGE TREE)

In its native habitat, *Cordyline australis* can form a tree of up to 10m (30ft), but in more northerly areas it usually reaches a height of about 2m (6ft), though if the conditions are exceptional it may reach 7m (21ft). In cold areas it is sometimes cut to the ground, but will shoot up again if the plant is well established. It produces elegant palm-like foliage (see opposite) and can look very good in coastal locations where it does well since it is resistant to strong winds and salt spray. Specimens of about ten or more years old will produce panicles of creamy-white flowers in summer. The trunk of the plant splays out at the base and has deep fissure-cracked bark.

It will tolerate temperatures as low as -10°C (14°F) and looks great on its own as an accent plant in a border or as a young plant with other exotic and tender plants such as salvia (see page 38), *Musa basjoo* (see page 31), echium (see page 36), canna (see page 41) and convolvulus (see page 59).

CULTIVATION

Site Selection In cold areas cordyline need a sunny position in well-drained soil. A south- or south-west-facing aspect is ideal. In partial shade, they grow a lot slower. They look good in containers as an accent plant in a group of pots and the coloured-leaved varieties are often used for this purpose. Plants used like this are best grown to the required size and then put in the container for the season.

Soil Cordyline don't mind what soil they are in as long as it is well drained. They can grow quite happily in heavy soil provided it doesn't get water-logged. If planting cordyline in a container, use a soil-based compost like John Innes No. 2.

Planting This is normally done in the late spring or early summer so that plants have the whole growing season to develop and settle in. They should be put in at the same depth as they were in the container. Take care when buying plants since those potted up in organic peat or coir-fibre compost will probably have developed a root system down to the bottom of the pot. When planting them out in the spring, it is a good idea to tap some of the compost away from the roots because that type of compost can absorb a lot of moisture in the winter and the roots may then rot. A handful of fertilizer like bonemeal in the bottom of the planting hole will give the cordyline a good start.

AFTERCARE

Feeding Cordyline require very little feeding and too much can promote lush growth which is then susceptible to winter cold and frosts. On alkaline soils, though, they can show signs of lime-induced chlorosis and it might be necessary to give them a dressing of a balanced slow-release fertilizer at the beginning of the year.

Pruning Very little pruning is required. Some people pull off the dead leaves which form around the base of the plant and this can give it a much tidier appearance. As plants get older they can form a twin stem or even three stems and indeed cordyline that reach a height of about 3m (10ft) will usually form a rosette of stems. The result of this is that the cold may attack and kill off a rosette and subsequently there will be several new stems, but dead wood can be cut out without any problems.

Winter Protection In cold districts it is wise to protect the crown of the plant by tying up all the leaves together and wrapping the plant in either horticultural fleece or bubble plastic. This will keep the frost out and prevent the plant from being damaged. You can also protect the base of the plant by giving it an organic mulch or again putting some

horticultural fleece round it and pegging it down with a few stones. This will help to stop the soil around the cordyline freezing. Cordyline can be cut to the ground by frosts, but in most cases they will sprout again in the spring.

Pests & Diseases Few pests and diseases affect cordyline, but sometimes the cultivated purple- and red-leaved forms get a rotting disease in cold weather which can reach down into the centre of the plant and destroy the growing tip. If this happens, the affected part should be cut out and the plant should be sprayed with a systemic fungicide. One other problem which may affect the leaves is a fungal disease that shows up in orange-brown patches. If this occurs, the worst of the leaves should be cut off and the plant should again be sprayed with a fungicide. If it looks as if this may affect new shoots in the spring, it might be worth introducing a spraying programme to keep the cordyline clean.

PROPAGATION

C. australis is usually propagated by seed, as is the species *C. indivisa*. Raising plants from seed is reasonably easy. The seed should be sown at a temperature of 18-21°C (65-70°F) in spring in a general seed compost. It should germinate quite quickly and the plants should be potted up before being put out in their second or third year.

It is not usual to take cuttings, although it can be done, and tall plants which have really outgrown their position can have the top 45cm (18in) cut off them which, if potted up and kept cool and partly shaded, may well root. This can take about three months.

OTHER VARIETIES

C. purpurea H & S: 2.5 x 1.5m (7 x 5ft). It has broader, arching leaves in a deep rich plum colour. *C. australis* 'Torbay Red' H & S: 1.5 x 1.5m (5 x 5ft). Has attractive greeny-bronze leaves with a bright red midrib. Neither of these varieties is as hardy as *C. australis*, so it is probably best to grow them in a container or lift them and take them inside during winter. *C. indivisa* H & S: 3 x 1.5m

(10 x 5ft). Has very broad leaves (up to 10cm [4in] across) which arch at the tips and which are browny green with a grey bloom on their underside. It is reputed to be as hardy as *C. australis*, if not hardier

Callistemon pallidus

(LEMON BOTTLE BRUSH)

A member of the myrtle family originating from Australia, the evergreen callistemon are actually a lot hardier than people think which is good news since they look superb in any garden. Provided it has a warmy, sunny and sheltered position, *Callistemon pallidus* will withstand temperatures of between -5°C (23°F) and -10°C (14°F) and *C. siberii* will occasionally survive temperatures of as low as -17°C (1°F). This is an evergreen shrub which can reach a height and spread of 2.1 x 1.25m (7 x 4ft).

The delightful lemon-coloured flowers of the callistemon are arranged around the stem and it is obvious why these give rise to the plant's common name (see page 52). Most of the other varieties produce flowers in shades of red and pink.

Callistemon look particularly good when grown next to other sun-loving plants from their part of the world such as eucalyptus, or the South American salvia (see page 38) or the fremontodendron (see page 58), agapanthus (see page 50) or ceanothus (see page 47). In cold districts they will do well in containers, but they only look their best in this situation when they are in flower.

CULTIVATION

Site Selection In their native Australia they tend to grow along the sides of streams and riverbeds, so they need a moisture-retentive soil, but it must be free-draining. Callistemon hate waterlogged conditions. A south- or southwest-facing wall suits them very well, in order for them to receive lots of reflected heat, though they should still do well in a border or a shrubbery. In warm, westerly coastal areas, callistemon can actually form a hedge since they will tolerate salt-laden winds and they make a good informal screen. They do, however, need direct sunshine for at least half the day.

Soil Any good garden soil will do for callistemon, provided they have good drainage. Heavy soils will certainly have to have their drainage improved.

Planting Young plants are normally planted in late spring or early summer in their final positions. They should be planted at the same depth as they were in the pot and watered in well.

AFTERCARE

Feeding A general fertilizer added to the surrounding soil should help newly-planted callistemon on their way. Established plants will benefit from a feed of liquid manure during the growing season. If planting in a container, give the shrub a weekly feed of liquid potash from late spring to late summer and then withhold it so the plant doesn't put on too much soft growth at the end of the year.

Pruning Pruning callistemon is quite straightforward. Newly-planted specimens should have their tips pruned to encourage them to bush up from the base. Established plants need only a light prune after flowering to keep them in check. Take out badly placed or crossing branches and cut back to strong growth by about a half. Less vigorous shoots can be cut back by about two thirds.

Winter Protection Callistemon may need a little bit of protection in very cold areas and this can be as simple as a piece of horticultural fleece draped over them, but in the right location winter protection shouldn't be a problem. If your garden is prone to strong easterly winds, it may be worthwhile erecting a netting screen around the plants to reduce the wind speed and prevent the cold burning the evergreen foliage. It may also help to give the plants a mulch of chopped bracken or straw to prevent the frost from reaching the roots.

Pests & Diseases Relatively pest and disease free, they may get scale insect on them which can be treated with a general insecticide at regular intervals from late spring to early summer. It is important to do this regularly over a period of time otherwise it won't have any effect on the insects.

PROPAGATION

Callistemon can be propagated by seed, although this does take a long time (often as long as a year), since the seed is slow to develop on the plant. The seed capsules are quite woody and they can stay on the plant for three to four years, usually opening up in the wild after forest and bush fires. Seed should be sown on the surface of a good compost in autumn or spring and the surface of the compost is must be kept permanently moist. Stand the seed pot in water up to about half its depth until the compost is thoroughly soaked, at a temperature of 15-18°C (60-65°F). If the compost dries up, replace the pot in the water. Don't water the seeds from above. With these requirements it is also necessary to have good air ventilation around the seeds and to keep them in a hygienic location to prevent any moulds breaking out on the compost. Do remember, if you are collecting your own seed, that callistemon hybridize freely in cultivation, so the seed you get may not be true to type.

An alternative method of propagation is by heeled, semi-ripe cuttings of lateral shoots in early to midsummer. If you take them in late summer to early autumn, they may need longer to establish. Put them in a closed case with some heat at the bottom at a temperature of 18-21°C (65-70°F). Dipping the cuttings in a hormone rooting powder also helps them to root.

OTHER VARIETIES

C. salignus (White or Willow Bottle Brush) H&S: 3 x 1.25m (10 x 4ft). It has broad, linear leaves with lots of dots on them and dense clusters of flowers which are mainly a greeny-white colour, although you can find pink and red varieties. *C. citrinus* H&S: 2 x 1.25m (6 x 4ft). This has silvery-red young shoots and bright red flowers.

Eremurus stenophyllus

(FOXTAIL LILY, DESERT CANDLE)

A very striking plant, eremurus tends to flower in spring, before the main rosette of leaves has grown. It has a very tall flower spike that grows to any-where between 1-1.5m (3-5ft) and is covered in many small white flowers which are tinged green at the centre. These two habits are responsible for the plant's common names, especially desert candle which refers to the way the eremurus seems to spring from nowhere out of the rocks with no leaves to herald its arrival. It makes a brilliant feature at the back of the border, towering over smaller plants (see page 53).

Originally from west and central Asia, the eremurus is fairly hardy, withstanding temperatures as low as -10°C (14°F), but like other plants in this chapter, it does hate the mixture of cold and wet.

CULTIVATION

Site Selection Eremurus like a sunny position. It doesn't have to be the warmest part of the garden, but they must have sun. Nor are they lovers of strong winds, and if this is a problem, they will have to be staked to avoid their flopping over and breaking.

Soil In the wild eremurus grow in semi-desert conditions in sandy soils. In wetter areas, it may be worth growing them in a raised bed or a slightly higher part of the garden so that they have a free-draining soil. Surprisingly the eremurus is quite a hungry plant as it needs a lot of nourishment to produce the large flower spike, so the soil should be reasonably fertile.

Planting Plants are usually put out in the spring and since the roots of the eremurus are quite fragile it is always best to buy young plants rather than old woody ones which will take longer to establish. When filling up the planting hole, once you get up to the crown it is a good idea to put a layer of sand or chippings around it to help prevent the crown from rotting in cold, wet winters. However, eremurus do appreciate dry, cold spells in winter which help them to flower well later on and poor flowering may be a problem in mild areas where the winters are warm and wet. Plant eremurus at the same depth as they were in their pots and water them in well. They can also benefit from a helping of fertilizer to aid their settling in.

AFTERCARE

Feeding A little bit of fertilizer should be hoed into the surrounding soil during spring, but eremurus do appreciate a mulch of rotted manure in late summer or early autumn which will give them a refreshing surge of nutrients to help them form clumps. This mulch should be cleared away before spring to prevent the moisture that it will attract from rotting the new emerging shoots.

Pruning Very little pruning is required. At the end of the season the dead leaf material should be pruned down to ground level and cleared away

Originating from the United States, the glorious yellow of Fremontodendron californicum *(opposite) adds a rich splash of colour to any garden.*

~

and, if you don't want seed, the flower spike can be cut off once flowering is over.

Winter Protection Eremurus need protecting not so much from the cold, but the wet, and in very wet areas it is worth working sharp sand into the soil around the crowns to help insulate them and make sure that any moisture drains away freely and doesn't rot them. In extreme conditions, you can put a cloche over the crowns to keep rains off.

Pests & Diseases This is a plant that is relatively free of pests and diseases, but again, in common with other leafy plants, it can attract slugs and snails.

PROPAGATION

Eremurus are normally propagated by seed which should be sown in the autumn. Alternatively, established crowns can be divided in the spring, but these may take a while to settle down again and the compost should be kept moist, though not too wet, while this is happening. Plants grown from seed may take about three to four years before they flower and seedlings should stay in their pots until they are large enough to handle.

OTHER VARIETIES

E. robustus H & S: 3 x 0.60m (10 x 2ft). A very large variety with a flowering head that can be anything up to 1m (3ft) long. The flowers are a delicate pink.

Fremontodendron californicum

(CALIFORNIAN GLORY, FLANNEL BUSH)

A semi-evergreen, *Fremontodendron californicum* is one of two fremontodendron species in cultivation, the other being *F. mexicanum*. They are natives of southwest North America and where the two are grown together they will produce hybrids. *F. californicum* really is a glorious plant bearing masses of large butter-yellow flowers from midsummer onwards until early autumn, which look lovely against the dark green leaves and stems which are covered in russet-coloured bristles (see opposite). Reaching a height and spread of 7 x 5m (21 x 15ft), it does very well against a warm wall where it will look good with other sun-lovers such as ceanothus (see page 47) or callistemon (see page 55) or more traditional climbers such as wisteria or *Campsis radicans*, the trumpet vine (see page 61). It is reasonably hardy, coping with temperatures down to around -15°C (5°F), but the hybrids do tend to do better than the individual species.

CULTIVATION

Site Selection As a lover of warmth and sun, the fremontodendron prefer a south- or southwest-facing aspect against a wall where the soil is well drained. In fact they are normally grown up against a wall or fence where they can be trained either as informal shrubs or more formally in fan shapes on guiding wires. The lateral branches are then pruned to form spurs. If grown away from a wall, they can make small free-standing shrubs.

Soil Fremontodendron like a free-draining soil. It doesn't have to be very fertile and in fact too rich a soil can result in them producing too much foliage and not enough flowers. They do well in shallow soils over chalk and in dry, sandy soils. Dry pockets of soil at the base of walls which are protected by overhanging roofs are ideal. Heavy soils will need improving dramatically to grow this plant well.

Planting Planting is normally done in late spring or early summer when the soil has had a chance to warm up and it should be thoroughly prepared. Fremontodendron don't have extensive roots systems, so if you are planting them against a wall, they can be positioned as little as 30cm (1ft) away without any problems. Put the plants in at the same depth as they were in their pots and water in well. Generally, these plants don't need a lot of water and will cope well in dry spells.

AFTERCARE

Feeding Fremontodendron need little feeding, but a light dressing of fertilizer hoed into the soil around the plants in spring can give them a boost. Plants grown in containers should occasionally receive a high-potash feed during the growing season, from late spring to midsummer.

Pruning The best time to prune is after flowering, usually in late summer, and fremontodendron really need just a light pruning to allow them to put on new growth and let light and air in to ripen the wood and encourage flower buds. If a fremontodendron is being trained in a fan shape against a wall, the lateral shoots should be pruned back to about three buds so that they can form spurs, rather as on an apple tree. Do take note that the bristles on the stems of fremontodendron can rub off very easily and, apart from covering your clothes, they can be inhaled, which causes irritation to some people, so use a face mask and gloves.

Winter Protection In cold areas plants may need a covering of horticultural fleece or netting. A 30-cm (12-in) mulch of chopped bracken will prevent the roots from freezing. Young plants should be protected until established.

Pests & Diseases Generally trouble-free.

PROPAGATION

Fremontodendron are usually propagated from seed which is best sown fresh in spring. It should be kept at a steady 21°C (70°F) and germination can be slow. Otherwise, these plants can be grown from softwood or semi-ripe cuttings in a sandy, well-drained, cutting mix rather than a heavier one which can rot the hairs on the stems. They need some heat at the bottom, so a propagator is ideal, and will help to overcome any problems in rooting.

OTHER VARIETIES

F. mexicanum H & S: 7 x 5m (21 x 15ft). It has broad, dark green leaves and russety hairs on the stems. It produces bright yellow, waxy-looking flowers in the summer. *F.* 'Ken Taylor' H & S: 5 x 4m (15 x 12ft). This has orange-yellow flowers which can appear right throughout the year. *F.* 'Pacific Sunset' H & S: 5 x 4m (15 x 12ft). This produces bright yellow flowers whose petal ends have short tail-like tips.

Convolvulus cneorum

(SILVER BUSH)

This delightful plant makes a lovely splash at the front of a sunny border or on a rock garden with its silky lanceolate leaves which are covered in grey hairs that give the plant a kind of silver sheen and pink buds that open into papery white flowers

with yellow throats which are borne in terminal clusters (see page 60). A native of the Mediterranean, *Convolvulus cneorum* can tolerate temperatures between -5°C (23°F) and -10°C (14°F) without too much trouble, as long as it's in a well-lit position. It will grow to a height of between 75 cm and 1 m (2½-3ft) and a spread of 1m (3ft), but it can be kept small by pruning to the required shape.

C. cneorum can look very good with other low-growing plants such as cytisus and helianthemum, and as part of a herbaceous border with plants like penstemon and salvia, especially *S. patens* and *S. guaranitica* (see page 38), where their contrasting blue flowers provide an excellent foil for the silver and white of the convolvulus. This plant can also look good grown in a container.

CULTIVATION

Site Selection *C. cneorum* needs an open sunny position in a well-drained soil, and in these conditions the plant should last between five and six years, after which it should be replaced.

Soil The convolvulus hates waterlogging, so if your soil is heavy it will need to be replaced as far as possible with a mixture of soils to aid drainage. *C. cneorum* doesn't need a particularly fertile soil and, if you are growing it in a container, it is a good idea to use a mixture of two thirds John Innes No. 2 and one third sharp grit to help drainage.

Planting It is best to plant convolvulus once the fear of frosts has passed in late spring and early summer when the plants can be put in their final position. They should be planted at the same depth as they were in the pot and, if they are looking a bit leggy, it is a good idea to pinch out some of the shoots to help them bush out.

AFTERCARE

Feeding Convolvulus don't need a lot of feeding and generally it is unnecessary, but if the plant is being grown in a container, it will need a weekly feed with a high-potash liquid fertilizer during the growing season from late spring to late summer. This will help keep the plant in tiptop condition.

Pruning Deadheading is perhaps the most important task, since it helps the plant to produce a succession of blooms. Generally, however, pruning is done simply to limit the plant's size and to take out any damaged or dead wood. It is best to prune after the convolvulus has finished flowering, so that the plant can settle in for the rest of the summer and form new growth.

Winter Protection In areas that suffer long spells of cold weather, it may be worth taking potted specimens indoors for the winter months. It is advisable to cover plants in the border with a sheet of horticultural fleece. Convolvulus don't like cold,

No garden should be without the silver-foliaged Convolvulus cneorum *with its delightful white flowers.*

~

easterly winds, so if your garden is prone to these, it is worthwhile erecting a small netting screen to protect the plants.

Pests & Diseases The convolvulus is not really susceptible to any particular pests or diseases.

PROPAGATION

Seed can be sown in the spring and kept at a steady 15-18°C (60-65°F). Otherwise it is possible to propagate convolvulus from semi-ripe, heeled cuttings in summer. These should be potted in a well-drained compost with moderate humidity over the top. It is also possible to take semi-ripe cuttings in late summer or early autumn and these will benefit from being dipped in a hormonel rooting powder and kept in a propagator with some heat at the bottom. This encourages quicker rooting and a sturdier rooting system. Plants can then be potted up and grown on.

OTHER VARIETIES

C. sabatius (formerly known as *C. mauritanicus* 'Sabatius') H&S: 30 x 60cm (12 x 48in). Lovely for the rock garden or for a trough or container. It has grey-green foliage and is covered in pale blue flowers during the summer months and sometimes early autumn. *C. althaeoïdes* H&S: 100 x 60cm (36 x 20in) This is more of a climber or trailing plant than a shrub in habit. It has grey-green leaves and broad pinky-purple flowers which are produced in the summer.

Campsis radicans

(TRUMPET VINE OR CREEPER)

A native of eastern North America, this really beautiful climber is used to growing in moist woodlands. If needs be, *Campsis radicans* can be grown as a bush or hedge, but is more commonly grown as a

~

The beautiful self-clinging climber Campsis radicans *looks its best when trailing over a wall with its profusion of elegant orange flowers.*

climber. It grows quite fast in the right conditions and has the ability to climb plants and walls aided by little clusters of adventitious roots that cling on to stonework and masonry and give it a strong adhesive power. It will reach a height and spread of 5 x 4m (15 x 12ft).

C. radicans can also be quite hardy, tolerating temperatures as low as -20°C (-4°F), but it does like a warm, sunny position, since without warmth it will not produce flower buds.

Campsis are deciduous and *C. radicans* has pinnate, light green leaves which provide a great backdrop for the beautiful trumpet-shaped flowers which can be scarlet or orange and as much as 7.5cm (3in) long and which appear in high summer.

CULTIVATION

Site Selection The best position for campsis is a south-facing wall or fence where they will receive full sun and protection from cold winds which they hate.

Soil Campsis are not too fussy about the type of soil they have, as long as it is well drained and moist. If they are planted in a very rich soil, there is a chance that they will put on too much growth at the expense of flowers. So, if the soil is heavy, they won't need a lot of feeding or mulching.

Campsis will be perfectly happy in thin chalky or sandy soils. But it is important that the soil doesn't dry out during the summer months. If it is prone to drought, then some well-rotted organic matter forked into the soil before planting will help retain moisture and a mulch can be put round the plant later on.

Planting Campsis should be planted out in early spring, bearing in mind the soil conditions as mentioned above. Depending on the plant's maturity, young growth should be tied to supports until the little aerial roots appear.

AFTERCARE

Feeding Campsis don't really require much feeding, but on alkaline soils they may suffer a little from lime-induced chlorosis and this can be rectified by feeding with a general liquid manure (with a high potash content, rather than a high nitrogen one) during the growing season.

Pruning Normally done in late winter or early spring, established plants should have the previous season's growth cut back to about two to three buds. Before plants mature they can be trained to a desired shape and size, and then leading shoots can be stopped and laterals allowed to grow as needed. Also, in the cases of older plants, dead wood will need to be removed.

Plants growing in dry areas will probably need just a light prune since growth will be much slower and only dead or diseased wood should have to be removed.

Winter Protection Very little winter protection is needed if the plant is grown in the right location.

Pests & Diseases Campsis can be affected by leaf spot or powdery mildew, which can be treated with a general fungicide. Scale insect, whitefly and mealy bug may cause problems in very warm areas or greenhouses when they can overwinter on the plants.

PROPAGATION

It is possible to propagate by seed which is quite straightforward, though it is worth noting that if *C. radicans* and the species, *C. grandiflora,* are growing next door to one another, hybridization will take place readily and offspring might not come true from seed. Seed should be sown at a temperature of 10-13°C (50-55°F) in spring. It is a good idea to stratify the seed first at a temperature of 5°C (41°F) for a couple of months in mid to late winter, as this will make germination more even.

Alternatively, one can take root cuttings 3-4cm (1½–2in) long in late winter which should be potted up in a closed case and kept at a temperature of 13-16°C (55-61°F).

Layering is another possibility. Arch longer branches down and peg them to the ground. Cover them in a few centimetres of soil and, by the end of the season they should have rooted into the ground and can be severed from the parent plant.

Cultivars are usually budded on to one-year-old seedling stock when they are dormant and *C. radicans* can also be propagated by hardwood cuttings in late autumn in a cold frame. These usually produce a heavy callus and root slowly. They should be lifted carefully and potted up the following spring.

OTHER VARIETIES

C. grandiflora H & S: 6 x 5m (18 x 15ft). A native of China and Japan, it is hardy down to -10°C (14°F). It flowers less densely than *C. radicans* and the blooms are more orange-coloured outside and yellow inside. *C.* x *tagliabuana.* H & S: 4 x 4m (12 x 12ft). This hybrid of *C. radicans* and *C. grandiflora* is quite shrubby in habit, with pinnate leaves that are

30cm (1ft) long. The flowers are orange on the outside and scarlet inside.

Trachycarpus fortunei

(CHUSEN PALM, CHINESE WINDMILL PALM)

A really beautiful plant, *Trachycarpus fortunei* can give any garden a really sub-tropical feel with its beautiful, ribbed, fan-shaped leaves (see page 13) which split at the ends and, including the leaf stalk, can be as long as 1m (3ft) and as wide as 75cm (2½ ft). It is modest in its growth, reaching a height of about 4-5m (12-15ft), and spreading to around 2m (6ft). It looks good when planted in groups of three, but a single specimen will provide an accent for any area.

As it grows, the young plant will form a dense cluster of foliage and then, after some years, it will form a single stem which is covered in a sort of woolly matting. Ten-to-fifteen-year-old plants will produce large panicles of golden-yellow flowers in late spring. Seed, though, is rarely formed, unless the plant is being grown under glass.

A native of China and Taiwan, this evergreen is usually found growing in mixed forests up to altitudes of 2400 m (7800 ft), so it can grow in cool conditions and will tolerate temperatures of as low as -10°C (14°F), although only for a short time.

CULTIVATION

Site Selection In order to do well trachycarpus like a west-, south- or southwest-facing aspect, where they can be warm and receive lots of sunshine. They are tolerant of winds, but it can shred the foliage, which gives the plants a dishevelled appearance, so the planting position needs to be quite sheltered too. It looks good in a mixed border or out on a lawn. If the proposed site is in a fairly cold location, then it is a good idea to plant it up against a warm wall or in a courtyard.

Soil The trachycarpus needs a free-draining, moisture-retentive soil, particularly in the summer. It is a myth that because most palms grow in the desert, they don't like water – they develop very long tap

roots to reach underground water sources. On the other hand palms will not tolerate waterlogged conditions.

Planting Young plants are normally planted in late spring or early summer, when the fear of frosts has passed and the soil has had a chance to warm up. If the plant is grown from seed, it is a good idea to keep it in its pot for two to three years to help it establish. Then it can be put out in its final position and watered in. It should settle down quite quickly and produce new foliage, but a clear stem won't really start to appear until the plant is about five to ten years old. When grown in a container, it needs an organic soil-based compost, such as John Innes No. 2, with a quarter of leaf mould or chopped bark and a helping of slow-release fertilizer added.

AFTERCARE

Feeding Trachycarpus require very little feeding, unless they are planted on very thin soils when they may show some signs of nutrient deficiency. In this case, they should be given a weak liquid feed at fortnightly intervals during the summer months.

Pruning Very little pruning is required. Old leaves turn yellow and eventually go brown and these should either be cut off leaving a short stub, or if pulled off, the whole plant can be tidied up and the hessian-like material can be pulled off too. But it is better to leave it on.

Winter Protection In very very cold districts trachycarpus in containers should be brought indoors, but in most gardens or sheltered locations, they can be left out where they are. If the winter does prove to be hard, it might be worth covering the crown with some horticultural fleece, to keep the worst of the cold off.

Pests & Diseases Generally trachycarpus are free from pests and diseases, though scale insect may be a problem under glass. And there are a couple of leaf spot diseases which can cause problems, but an application or two of a systemic fungicide should clear them up.

PROPAGATION

Usually palms are propagated by seed and they germinate quickly. Since the seed has such a short shelf life, it is best sown when it is fresh. Sow it in a sandy loam in a propagating frame and keep it at a temperature of about 24°C (75°F). Seedlings should be pricked out and potted on for a further couple of years under glass. They can then be hardened off in a cold frame before being transferred outside.

OTHER VARIETIES

T. wagnerianus H & S: 7 x 1m (21 x 3ft). This handsome species is similar to *T. fortunei* in many ways and just as hardy, but its leaves are smaller – around 45cm (1½ft) – and very stiff and leathery. And whereas the leaf tips of *T. fortunei* tend to go brown and fray, those of *T. wagnerianus* will stay green and sturdier for longer.

MORE HARDY SUN-LOVING PLANTS TO TRY

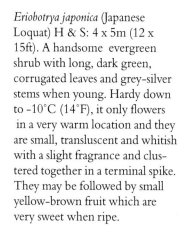

Acca sellowiana (Pineapple Guava) H & S: 4 x 2.5m (12 x 7ft). An evergreen shrub, it has dark green leaves which are almost silver on the back. Its young stems are also covered in silver hairs. Flowers appear in late summer and are a rosy red-purple with fleshy petals. Hardy down to -10°C (14°F), it makes an excellent plant for coastal gardens.

Carpenteria californica (Tree Anemone) H & S: 3 x 4m (9 x 12ft). A delightful evergreen shrub from California with dark, olive-green foliage that has a silvery-white sheen to the back of the leaves. White flowers with a deep yellow centre are produced in summer and the petals are papery in texture. It is hardy down to -10°C (14°F).

Cestrum parqui (Willow-leaved Jasmine) H & S: 3 x 2m (9 x 6ft). A deciduous hairy shrub with long arching stems. Its leaves are long, narrow and light green. The yellowish-green tubular flowers are produced freely in terminal clusters from mid-summer through to autumn, often lasting until the first frost. It is hardy down to -10°C (14°F).

Eriobotrya japonica (Japanese Loquat) H & S: 4 x 5m (12 x 15ft). A handsome evergreen shrub with long, dark green, corrugated leaves and grey-silver stems when young. Hardy down to -10°C (14°F), it only flowers in a very warm location and they are small, transluscent and whitish with a slight fragrance and clustered together in a terminal spike. They may be followed by small yellow-brown fruit which are very sweet when ripe.

Fuschia microphylla H & S: 2 x 1m (6 x 3ft). This bushy, Central American, evergreen shrub has strong branches with minute, dark, glossy leaves. Flowers can be produced at any time of year, but are particularly common in late summer or early autumn. They are small, tubular and cerise, purple or occasionally white in colour. It will tolerate some dappled shade and is hardy down to -15°C (5°F).

Mandragora officinarum (Mandrake) H & S: 30 x 100cm (1 x 3ft). A Mediterranean plant shrouded in superstition, this herbaceous perennial has long ovate leaves which dry off in summer when the plant is in its dormant period. Flowers appear very early in the year at ground level. They are borne in a loose rosette and are papery yellow with a purple centre; they are followed by round fruit which turn yellow when ripe and are poisonous. It is hardy down to -10°C (14°F).

Punica granatum (Pomegranate) H & S: 2 x 1.5m (6 x 5ft). A small to medium-sized deciduous shrub with glossy, dark green leaves that are bronze when young. Its flowers are bright orange-red and silky and appear in summer. Hardy down to -10°C (14°F), it also produces brown-yellow fruits of about 12cm (5in) in diameter.

Solanum crispum 'Glasnevin' H & S: 4 x 3m (12 x 9ft). A vigorous deciduous shrub with small, matt green, oval leaves which are rather malodorous. Its flowers are lilac to deep purple in colour with bright yellow stamens and they are produced in large clusters throughout the summer. It is hardy down to -10°C (14°F).

Desert Plants

~

Nothing can be more spectacular in a garden in northern climates than a plant which looks as though it came straight from the tropics or a desert island, and the plants in this chapter will certainly give any garden such an impression. With their strong foliage and unusual flowers, any of these plants will provide a talking point for you and your friends. Oddly, it is not actually the heat that keeps the desert plants going, it is the fact that they are kept dry. The agave, dasylirion and opuntia all come from the deserts of the southern USA and Mexico, while the fascicularia, ochagavia and the puya all originate from high up in the Andes mountains of South America. All these regions can be very cold with temperatures that frequently fall below freezing, but the plants thrive because of the aridity of their surroundings.

It will be obvious, then, that what these plants hate most is winter moisture which can cause rotting

~

Full sun and shelter are important for plants like the spiky Yucca flaxoniana *(page 71), centre left, the rosette-forming* Ochagavia carnea *(page 74), front and centre, and the sea urchin-like grey-green,* Puya berteroniana *(page 78), front and left of white daisies.*

and allow them to succumb to the cold. During the summer they can be watered as often as is needed, though a normal summer rainfall is usually enough to meet their requirements.

SITE SELECTION

Keeping plants like these dry out in the garden during the winter might seem a tall order, but it can be done. In my garden in the West Country most of the wet weather comes in from the Atlantic, so the east side of the house is in a rain shadow and, in fact, the border up against the house hardly ever gets any direct rain at all. And although this side of the building is cooler and more exposed to easterly winds, the desert plants that I grow there don't seem to mind because they are kept dry.

If you can't plant on one side of a building or another, then try planting the desert plants at the base of a garden wall (south-facing is best) or in a raised bed or terrace. If you have a broad natural stone wall in your garden, you could try planting on top of it by placing the plants between the stones and adding some grit around them. The plants will love this and they can easily be covered in winter. But wherever you choose, do ensure that the plants are in the sunniest position possible and that the soil is very free-draining.

SOIL

Drainage is, of course, the key factor when it comes to growing these desert plants. In fact, it is probably best to plant them in pockets composed almost entirely of grit or gravel. About eight years ago I planted some puya and ochagavia and before putting the soil back round the roots I mixed in some sharp grit which was the equivalent of at least three quarters of the amount of soil. I also put a layer of grit in the base of the hole and mulched round the plants with it as well. That may seem a bit excessive, but it has paid off. Each plant has at least doubled in size and they all flower on a regular basis. None of them has rotted off despite their growing outside during cold, wet winters. The grit has provided just the right amount of drainage and the mulch has given the crown good drainage too, as well as insulating the ground underneath.

If your soil is quite sandy and free-draining, you won't need to add so much grit, but those of you with heavy, wet, clay soils may find that no amount of grit or gravel will allow you to establish these plants successfully. All is not lost, though, because you can remove the soil from the area in which you wish to grow your desert plant and mix up your own soil to backfill the hole around the plant.

PLANTING

The best time to plant is usually spring when the threat of frost has passed and the soil has had time to warm up. Choose a dry day when the soil is not saturated, otherwise it will be more difficult to mix in the grit. If the soil is just moist, it will mix easily and be easier to use for backfilling around the roots of the plant. Always water the plants in well after planting, but frequent watering of desert plants is not necessary even during dry spells. It is far better to let their roots grow down and find their own water.

WINTER PROTECTION

Provided you have chosen the right place for your plants, you will seldom need to give them any protection in winter. But plants that are experiencing their first winter may need some form of cover. It allows them to settle in and not suffer any setbacks which they may well do if the winter is long and cold. A simple layer of polythene around the base of the plant and sloping away from it will help to deflect excess moisture and a double layer of horticultural fleece laid over the top and held down with some stones will protect the crown. Don't mulch the plants with chopped bark or any similar material as this will absorb too much water and could cause them to rot.

Agave americana

(CENTURY PLANT)

Agave are a large genus of plants which originate from the southern states of North America, Mexico and the northern parts of South America. They are generally a striking-looking group of succulent

66

perennials and *Agave americana* is no exception. Used by native American Indians as food and for brewing some rather fearsome alcoholic drinks from the sap, agave are better known in Europe as the origin of sisal, especially *A. sisalana*.

The common name arises from the myth that it takes around a hundred years for the plant to flower. In fact even the slowest agave will flower somewhere around the 30- or 40-year mark and smaller species can flower within six to eight years from seed. But the larger species do tend to be monocarpic in that they put all their energies into producing the one tall flower spike from the main rosette which will die after the flowers and seeds have been produced. However, numerous small rosettes will have been produced around the base for new plants and so losing the older plant is not necessarily a problem.

A. americana can reach a height of 1.5m (5ft) with leaves that can get as long as 1.25m (4ft). It produces beautiful rosettes of grey-green leaves (see page 68) and, when the time is right, a flower spike of about 5-7m (15-20ft) which is covered in yellow-green flowers. It will tolerate a temperature as low as -4°C (25°F), but only for a short time and only if its roots are dry. The agave looks good with yucca (see page 71), cordyline (see page 53) and bulbs like nerine (see page 45) and agapanthus (see page 50).

CULTIVATION

Site Selection Given their origins, agave really need impeccable drainage, so planting them at an angle on a raised bed or slope is best, and coastal districts are often good locations. Ideally, they should be placed in a warm, sunny and generally frost-free position, but if your garden is susceptible to frosts, then the best thing is to grow agave in a container. It can then stand in great splendour either on the patio or in the border and be taken indoors before the frosts start.

Soil Agave don't like excessively rich soils as they can promote too much lush growth. They prefer soils of moderate fertility, such as a well-drained, sandy soil.

Planting This is normally done in the spring once the fear of frosts has passed. The soil should be well-prepared, particularly if it is heavy, in which case the drainage needs to be improved dramatically, or else the plant will rot. Alternatively, you could remove the soil in the planting area to an extent of about 360sq. cm (4sq. ft) and backfill it with a free-draining compost. In this situation, though, it may be best to plant the agave in a container. If you do, use a compost such as John Innes No. 2 with a third of the mixture consisting of a sharp grit or a soil improver, such as vermiculite or perlite, to help drainage. In situations where they might be prone to water settling on the leaves and crown, agave should be planted at an angle so that the water can drain off.

Plant the agave at the same depth as it was in its pot. When you knock the plant out of the pot, you may find that there are a lot of young plantlets developing round the base. These can easily be cut off, or left to mature if you prefer.

AFTERCARE

Feeding Agave generally require very little feeding – even plants that have spent a long time in containers and become pot-bound don't seem to suffer and may indeed be encouraged to produce flowers. But they will benefit from a feed of liquid fertilizer that is low in nitrogen and high in potassium and potash during the growing season.

Pruning Very little pruning is required, but plants that are handled regularly or positioned where people, and especially children, are likely to brush up against them should have the needle-like ends of their leaves removed as they can be dangerous.

Old leaves will eventually turn yellow and wither. They can stay on the plant for several years around the base, but once they have shrivelled up and turned brown you can cut them off with a sharp knife to tidy up the plant.

Winter Protection The best winter protection, if your garden is prone to frost, is to keep agave very dry and to store them in a cool greenhouse or conservatory during the winter months.

The majestic grey-green Agave americana *provides the perfect backdrop for its relative, the variegated* Agave americana *'Marginata'.*

~

If the plant is situated in a bed, then it is a good idea to cover it with some horticultural fleece and the surrounding soil with a polythene sheet (to keep the rain off) in cold snaps and to insulate it by packing the agave round with straw underneath the sheet.

Pests & Diseases Agave are prone to very few pests and diseases, but mealy bug can be a problem for plants coming out of greenhouses.

The disease that causes most trouble is a fungus known as penny spot which affects agave badly in winter months. Still, cool, dank air encourages the fungus which produces large spots on the leaves that rot and eventually die. They make the plant look most unsightly. For some reason variegated leaf forms appear to be more prone to this than the plain green varieties. A regular application of a systemic fungicide should keep plants clean and prevent them from getting penny spot.

PROPAGATION

Agave are very easy to propagate. You can tap mature plants out of their pots, or lift them, and break off young plantlets which develop around their bases. Once these are potted up they will produce roots very quickly and grow away happily.

In the wild, agave produce abundant seed, but it is more difficult to get hold of in more northerly, colder climates. If you do manage to collect any seed, it should be sown immediately. It takes as long as two months to germinate and should be kept at a steady 13-15°C (55-60°F).

OTHER VARIETIES

A. americana 'Marginata' H & S: 1.5 x 1.25m (5 x 4ft). It has leaves widely edged with yellow. *A. americana* 'Variegata' H & S: 1.25 x 1m (4 x 3ft). Its leaves are edged with white. Both varieties are extremely attractive and their rosettes can get quite big – around 2m (6ft) – and they should both be wintered indoors. *A. victoriae-reginae* H & S: 60 x 40cm (48 x 16in). It has stout, olive green leaves edged with silvery white which grow to about 25cm (10in) long. This species looks very attractive grown in a container. It is a native of Mexico and, while quite tough, should be kept at a minimum of 5°C (41°F) during the winter.

Opuntia compressa

(PRICKLY PEAR)

If you really want to impress your gardening friends and neighbours, the opuntia is the plant to go for. This large genus of cacti which are native to the southern United States, Mexico and Central America are divided into two groups. One group is found in the lowland areas and is sub-tropical in nature prefering a minimum temperature of 5-10°C (41-50°F).

The other group is found at much higher altitudes and can therefore tolerate lower temperatures, such as -5°C (23°F), for short periods, but like the rest of the genus it needs dry conditions. So, if you can provide a good, dry position in the garden, you should be able to grow one of the hardier varieties of opuntia.

Opuntia compressa belongs to the latter group and has in fact naturalized in some parts of Switzerland, although it originates from the eastern and central United States.

It is fairly small, reaching a height and spread of 20 x 30cm (8 x 12in) and it produces yellow flowers in the summer (see below). These are followed by small, fleshy, purple-red fruits which are 2.5-5cm (1-2in) in length and which appear on the succession of small, flat pads that make up each stem.

O. compressa looks most attractive when planted with yucca (see page 71), sedum, sempervivum and agave (see page 66).

One of the most interesting species of the cacti family, the succulent stems of the opuntia are flattened in to broad pads which act as water reservoirs in times of drought. These pads give the plant a unique apearance and in summer they are crowned by the brightest of flowers as this Opuntia compressa *shows here.*

CULTIVATION

Site Selection Opuntia really need to be grown somewhere where they are protected as much as possible from the rain. So up against a wall where there is an overhanging roof would be ideal. Generally, though, it is difficult to protect them totally from the wet and in an open border you will probably find that during the winter the bottom of the stem will get wet and rot. If this does happen, it can be cut off in the spring and the next healthy section pushed into the ground where I've found it roots without too many problems.

In addition to this protection, opuntia also need warmth, sunshine, good air movement and free drainage, which is most important. They don't mind the cold in winter as long as they have excellent drainage – a raised bed or embankment would be best.

Soil Since drainage is so important, a soil that is quite gritty and stony is ideal. Any soil that gets waterlogged will present problems. If your soil verges on this type, then it is a good idea to remove soil from the planting spot up to an area of 2025sq. cm (2¼sq. ft) and backfill the hole with free-draining soil or a mixture of 60 per cent John Innes No. 2 and 40 per cent sharp grit.

Planting Opuntia should be planted in the spring, once the fear of frosts has passed, at the same depth as they were in their pots. One problem with handling opuntia is their spines which can be particularly nasty if they pierce your hands. A good way of getting to grips with them is to take two quite thick rolls of old newspaper and place them either side of a plant, so that you can pick it up without hurting yourself. Water the plants in well and after that they are really quite undemanding for the rest of the season.

AFTERCARE

Feeding Opuntia don't need much feeding, but a helping of a high-potash fertilizer can keep them in good condition, though they shouldn't need much if they are outside in the garden. If you feed cacti too much, they can become soft and put on a lot of lush growth which makes them prone to winter damage.

Pruning A very straightforward matter, since opuntia need hardly any pruning. Dead or damaged pads can be cut off to keep the plant tidy. In these cases a secondary, lateral pad may form which may make the plant top-heavy. If this happens, the new pad can be either left or cut off and used for propagation, or you can stake the plant.

Winter Protection The main problem is to protect opuntia from the wet rather than the cold which they can usually tolerate. A cloche is a good idea and will keep off the worst of the winter moisture, or you could place potted plants in a cool, dry greenhouse.

Pests & Diseases Few things trouble opuntia, except for mealy bug whose sugary deposits can be colonized by a sooty mould which makes plants look unsightly. If the affected area is quite small, it can be dabbed with a paintbrush dipped in surgical spirit which will kill off the mealy bug. If the infestation is more widespread, use a general insecticide.

PROPAGATION

Opuntia are quite simple to propagate. Seed should be sown thinly on the top of compost and kept at a steady 21°C (70°F). It will germinate quite quickly. Seedlings can be pricked off when they are large enough to handle and potted up, but they shouldn't be put outside until their third year, otherwise they may succumb to damage.

It is also possible to propagate opuntia by cutting off a pad (a portion of the stem) and burying the bottom 25 per cent of it in a cutting mixture which is open and free-draining. You don't need to wound the cutting or to dip it in hormone rooting powder. In fact, when the pad is cut off, it should be left in the sun for a few hours so that the cut can dry. This will help to prevent any rot getting into the cutting. Rooting can be a bit slow and may take anything between two and three months to establish properly. Once it has rooted, the cutting can be potted up in a mixture of John Innes No. 2 and sharp grit as previously mentioned and grown on for a short while before being planted out or put in its final-size pot.

OTHER VARIETIES

O. cantabriginensis H & S: 20 x 30cm (8 x12in). A hybrid raised at the University of Cambridge Botanic Gardens, this has large pads of between 18-25cm (7-10in) in width which are grey-green and covered in longish white spines. The flowers are yellow and produced in summer. *O. humifusa* H & S: 20 x 10cm (8 x 4in). It is a bright, fresh, oak-coloured green and has small clusters of spines on it. The flowers that are produced in spring are yellow and cluster at the ends of the pads. It is quite hardy, provided it is kept dry at the roots

Yucca flaxoniana

Although most commonly grown as houseplants, yucca are also popular in the garden, providing a strong focus for any suitable location.There are various species to suit every size of garden. Some can grow quite tall, such as *Y. gloriosa* which can reach up to 2m (6ft) and has long, dark green, almost black, leaves. But *Yucca flaxoniana* is one of the smaller varieties and is slightly different from most yucca because it tends to have fewer leaves which are thick and fleshy. In addition, the fibres along the edges of the leaves split off, forming tassles which give this yucca an unusual appearance (see page 65). It can reach a height of 60cm (2ft) and a spread of 80cm (32in) with leaves as long as 45-60cm (18-24in). *Y. flaxoniana* is also quite hardy, tolerating temperatures down to about -5°C (23°F), providing it has a sunny, sheltered position. It is a slow grower and, like the dasylirion (see page 72), will look well with silver-foliaged plants as well as many of the plants mentioned in this chapter.

CULTIVATION

Site Selection Yucca prefer warm, sunny conditions. They don't mind winds, as long as they aren't too cold. Terraced beds or rock gardens where the conditions are dry or the corner of a patio which receives a lot of sun are good situations. If you live in a very cold area, though, you might consider growing yucca in a container, so that it can be put out during the summer months and then overwintered in a greenhouse or conservatory.

Soil These plants need a very free-draining soil, but one which retains a little moisture and is rich and loamy. They will tolerate poor, sandy soils and in colder areas, these have the benefit of discouraging too much growth that is susceptible to frost damage.

If your garden tends to get quite wet, it is a good idea to plant the yucca on a slope or embankment or even a wall, and if you need to replace the soil in the planting area then use a mixture of half John Innes No. 2 and half sharp grit. Having the right soil around the crown is particularly important, since any excess moisture will cause the plant to rot.

Planting Yucca are normally planted out in mid to late spring. Water the plants in well and keep them watered until they are established. Normally they will have no problem in sending down their roots to find moisture in the soil. The yucca's roots are quite thick and will eventually form what are known as 'toes', which produce plantlets that come up near the base of the plant or even some distance away. If this happens, it shows that the plant is happy, and if the plantlets are left, they will form a clump around the parent plant which looks very attractive.

AFTERCARE

Feeding At planting time, you can add a little general fertilizer to the surrounding soil, but not too much because the yucca doesn't need a great deal. Specimens grown in containers should be given a weak liquid feed that is high in potash and low in nitrogen fertilizer once a fortnight during the growing season, which should then be stopped in winter.

Pruning Yucca will almost tell you when they need pruning, which is very rarely. Old leaves will shrivel and turn yellow before dying. These can be pulled off, but before you do so make sure they are really dead, in which case you can twist them off and they should come away cleanly. It is a good idea to remove the dead material since it can encourage disease.

Winter Protection As long as yucca are in the right position and have the right type of soil, they should not need any winter protection, but in very cold areas you might want to wrap them up in some horticultural fleece to keep the worst of the winter cold away. Don't wrap them in polythene as this can make them sweat which will also encourage disease and the plants will rot.

Pests & Diseases Yucca are prone to some leaf-spotting diseases. The most common is evidenced by concentric brown rings that appear on the leaves and which can develop quite rapidly during the autumn and winter months and make the plant look very unsightly. If these rings do appear, cut off the diseased areas and either burn them or put them in the dustbin. Don't put them on the compost heap. Then spray the yucca with a copper-based fungicide to prevent the fungi from recurring. Generally, yucca grown outside don't suffer from pests, but plants which are overwintered indoors may suffer the odd attack of mealy bug.

PROPAGATION

Normally yucca are propagated by seed which is difficult to collect yourself as you would need to hand-pollinate the flowers, but it is available commercially. It will germinate in 8-10 weeks and should be kept at 15-18°C (60-65°F).

OTHER VARIETIES

Y. filifera 'Golden Sword' H & S: 1.5 x 1.25m (5 x 4ft). Its leaves are 0.5m (1½ft) long with yellow leaf margins and its flower spike reaches 1.5m (5ft) in height and has many small pendant white flowers. *Y. whipplei* H & S: 0.5 x 1m (1½-3ft). This has narrow, needle-like leaves that are grey-green in colour and produces a flower spike of about 3m (10ft) with fleshy pendulous blooms that are a white-cream colour. It is good for the small garden or for growing in a container.

Dasylirion acrotrichum

(BEAR GRASS)

In its native Mexico this member of the agave family can reach tree-like proportions – often as high as 1.5-2m (5-6ft) and spreading as wide as 1.2m (4ft). Similar to a yucca, it has masses of striking long, thin, almost needle-like leaves which radiate out from the top of the trunk and make it look like a sea urchin. The end of each leaf splits, giving it a tufted appearance, and along the leaf edge there are sharp curved spines which are pale yellow in colour. These leaves can be as long as 1m (3ft) and are about 2cm (¾in) wide.

Dasylirion are monocarpic (i.e. they die after flowering), but it takes a long time for a flower spike to appear – up to 20 years. This can be as tall as 4½m (13ft). When it does it is usually in summer and the spike is covered in dense bracts of small, white, cylindrical flowers.

With its strong architectural appearance, the dasylirion looks good when planted with other similarly shaped plants such as the agave (see page 66), cordyline (see page 53) or yucca (see page 71), or even the trachycarpus (see page 63). Alternatively, it will look very effective if placed amongst silver-leaved plants like *Stachys lanata* or any artemisia and especially *Eryngium maritimum* and *E. variifolium*. These can give a garden a real Mediterranean appearance.

These plants can tolerate quite cool conditions, down to about 0°C (32°F), but in very cold areas it is probably best to grow them in pots and overwinter them in a greenhouse or cold frame.

CULTIVATION

Site Selection Dasylirion need very dry, sunny conditions and I have seen an example grown in a wall which provides ideal drainage. They will do well in any coastal garden and also in a raised or terraced bed.

~

The large, round, sea-urchin appearance of Dasylirion acrotrichum *provides a unique focus for a dry, sunny position.*

Soil A free-draining, soil is best and it won't do any harm to add in some more grit and sand. Avoid rich soils because these will encourage the dasylirion to put on too much soft growth.

Planting Young plants should be put out once the fear of frosts has passed. They should be planted at the same depth as they were in their pots and watered in well. Be careful not to let any compost fall in the base of the leaves as this will store moisture and could cause the dasylirion to rot. It will be very apparent if this happens, because the leaves will start to collapse and the plant will lose its sea-urchin look. After the growing season watering should be decreased so that plants can begin to dry out and go into their dormant period which lasts from early autumn to the beginning of spring. If planting the dasylirion in a container, use two parts of a compost such as John Innes No. 2 (which does not have too much fertilizer in it) and one part grit or sharp sand.

AFTERCARE

Feeding Generally, dasylirion need very little feeding. Plants in containers can be given a liquid feed that is high in potash and low in nitrogen (which should not be totally absent) to keep them looking their best. But don't feed them more than about once a fortnight. If they are overfed, as mentioned in the section on soil, they can put on too much lush growth and will then be prone to attack from frost.

Pruning Many people tend to leave the dead foliage around the base of the plant to give it a natural appearance, but if you feel it looks unsightly or it is likely to attract the damp and therefore rot, then you can either pull or cut it off near the trunk.

Winter Protection As mentioned, if you live in a very cold area, then winter protection is essential. Both the roots and the crown need to be kept dry. In this case, it is a good idea to put a polythene covering around the base of the plant and angled away from it so that any water will drain off. Otherwise, specimens grown in containers can be brought indoors and kept in a well-lit and well-ventilated position.

Pests & Diseases Dasylirion are subject to very few problems, but they may suffer a bit from mealy bug while under glass.

PROPAGATION

This is normally done by seed which should be sown when fresh in the spring. It should germinate quite quickly if kept at a temperature of about 18°C (65°F). When the seedlings are large enough to handle – about 7.5cm (3in) high – you should pot them up individually since they have quite a large tap root. Unlike agave, dasylirion don't produce plantlets, so raising them from seed is the most reliable way of propagation.

OTHER VARIETIES

D. wheeleri H & S: 1.5 x 1m (5 x 3ft). A small bushy tree with leaves that are slightly shorter than those of *D. acrotrichum*, but wider – 2-4cm (¾-1½in) – and they have small hooked spines on them that are yellow to rusty brown in colour. A native of southern Arizona and Texas, it produces a flower spike of 2.5-5m (7½-15ft) which is covered in small white-yellow flowers. But flowering is rare in cultivation and *D. wheeleri* is normally grown simply for its foliage. It is also less hardy than *D. acrotrichum* and is only cultivated outside in frost-free localities.

Ochagavia carnea

The ochagavia is a member of the Bromeliad family most of which grow as epiphytes (commonly known as 'air plants', they spend their lives growing on tree branches, taking moisture from the air) and which do best in tropical conditions. This rather fierce-looking plant is a geophyte which grows in the ground and one of a very few which will survive in more northern climates. It is usually found on the coasts of central Chile.

Ochagavia carnea is quite large, reaching a spread of 60cm (2ft), and forming dense mounds of rosettes with large, spiny-edged leaves that are usually about 20cm (8in) long (see page 65).

They look very good amongst rocks and will survive in pockets of almost pure gravel. A good feature for all-year round interest in the garden, they look dramatic when planted with yucca (see page 71), puya (see page 78) and cordyline (see page 53) or silver-foliaged plants like artemisia, helichrysum and *Convolvulus cneorum* (see page 59).

Plants will only flower when they are mature enough, but it is quite a spectacular sight. Nestling in the rosette, the large mound (often as big as 8cm [3½in]) of small white buds opens up into scaly pinky-lavender flowers which become papery and transparent. The ochagavia will tolerate temperatures as low as -10°C (14°F) for short periods.

CULTIVATION

Site Selection Ochagavia require a sheltered, dry situation with very good drainage in full sun. The base of a wall under an overhanging roof is a good place for them. But they will also do well in a rock garden or raised bed or even a dry stone wall which has been backfilled with gritty soil.

Soil Don't put the ochagavia in a peat- or coir-based compost mixture because this will retain too much moisture. They prefer a gritty, free-draining soil and if you need to improve the soil in the area where you want to plant it, you should add as much as 60 per cent grit to a depth of about 45cm (18in).

Planting This is normally done in spring and the ochagavia should be planted at the same depth as it was in its pot and watered in well until it is established. After that it doesn't really need any special watering. In very cold areas, you might prefer to plant the ochagavia in a pot, in which case it will need a similar potting mixture to the fascicularia (see page 76) and occasional watering. If you do plant it outside, though, placing the plant at an angle is a good idea, since this will allow excess moisture to run off and away from the crown. Put a heavy mulch of gravel – about 8cm (3in) – around the base of the plant as well, as this will also help drainage and provide some insulation.

AFTERCARE

Feeding It is not really a good idea to feed this plant when it is outside, because it can promote too much lush foliage which will be susceptible to the cold. Container-grown specimens, however, may have the occasional liquid feed, which is high in potash and low in nitrogen, during the growing season, but don't give it too much.

Pruning The ochagavia doesn't need much pruning, but the dead leaves do need taking off and this is quite difficult, since the spines on the leaves can catch hold of gardening gloves and fingers, so it can be rather a slow job. The best thing to do is wait until the leaves are really dried up and then pull them off. It is time-consuming but worth doing as the plant will look much neater.

Winter Protection Wrap the ochagavia in a couple of sheets of horticultural fleece, but not polythene as this will make the plant sweat and so encourage diseases. In very cold areas, you might consider putting up a glass frame over it as protection from the worst of the winter wet. Plants in pots and containers can be put in a frost-free greenhouse or conservatory for the winter.

Pests & Diseases The usual sort of leaf spots can occur and by the end of the winter the plants can look a bit shabby. The ochagavia should soon grow out of this, but if you want to keep the plant looking perfect all the way through the winter then spray it with a systemic fungicide in the autumn. Pests aren't really a problem.

PROPAGATION

You can divide mature ochagavia and pot up the rosettes. If you leave them on the dry side, they should establish new roots after a couple of months. Otherwise, it is possible to grow ochagavia from seed. Seed should be sown fresh, if possible, and should barely be covered. It will germinate in about two months if kept at a temperature of 13-15°C (55-60°F). Plants grown from seed will take quite a long time to flower, though, so you need to be patient if you use this method of propagation.

Mature, container-grown specimens can be taken out and divided. You will often find small plantlets, like suckers, at the base of the parent plant and these can be broken off and potted up.

OTHER VARIETIES

Although there are five species of the genus *O. carnea* is the only one in cultivation.

Fascicularia pitcairniifolia

Originating from central and southern Chile, this wonderful plant is another member of the Bromeliad family and like the ochagavia is a geophyte. It will tolerate temperatures as low as -10°C (14°F) or -15°C (5°F) for short periods.

Giving the appearance of a large clump of grass, the fascicularia has beautiful, long, dark green leaves whose bases turn a bright pillar-box red around the flowers that grow deep inside the rosettes, in order to attract pollinators. The flowers are a beautiful pinky-turquoise and bloom in the late summer, making quite a feature when many other plants will already have finished their flowering season. It is a slow-growing plant: the clump will only reach a spread of 75-100cm (2½-3ft) after many years, while the leaves can reach a height of 1m (3ft), but on average usually grow as tall as 60cm (2ft).

The fascicularia will look good with many of the other plants in this chapter, particularly the yucca (see page 71) or the dasylirion (see page 72), but it will also complement other hardy desert-looking succulent plants, such as sedum and sempervivum and silver-foliaged plants like artemisia and helichrysum.

CULTIVATION

Site Selection This plant needs very dry conditions and excellent drainage, especially during the winter. Don't worry about a lack of moisture because the fascicularia has long roots which it sends down into the ground to find what it needs. It will do well in a raised or terraced bed or a rock garden. And, if it is planted at an angle, on a bank for example, its flowers can be seen to advantage.

Soil As drainage is so important, you may need to replace the soil in the growing area with a mixture that includes a lot of grit. A good mixture would consist of about 40 per cent John Innes No. 2 soil-based compost and 60 per cent grit or sharp sand. Or you could even grow the fascicularia in a bed where the top 30cm (1ft) is pure gravel. The same mixtures can be used if you are planting the fascicularia in a pot, but don't use all gravel as this species does need to be able to reach some nutrients.

Planting Fascicularia should be put out in the spring when the ground is beginning to warm up. Make sure the soil has been prepared as described above and plant the fascicularia at the same depth as it was in its pot and water it in well.

AFTERCARE

Feeding Fascicularia need very little feeding. If the plant is growing on a chalky, alkaline soil, it may show signs of lime-induced chlorosis, in which case a little general fertilizer will help to rectify this.

Pruning Again, the fascicularia shouldn't have to be pruned very much. Dead leaves can be taken off and this is usually necessary in late spring. Sometimes, though, the top 10cm (4in) or so of the leaves are killed by frost which gives the fascicularia rather an ugly appearance. If this happens, cut these sections off in spring, down to where the tissue is healthier, and the plant will look much neater.

Winter Protection If you live in a really cold area, you may want to cover the fascicularia with some horticultural fleece, particularly if it is relatively young. Generally, however, these plants will tolerate frost, though if the winter is hard, you may have to take off quite a bit of dead foliage in spring.

Pests & Diseases Occasionally, these plants get a little bit of leaf-spotting which they should normally grow out of, but to keep them really clean you could spray them with a general fungicide. Apart from that fascicularia are usually free of pests and diseases. Damaged leaves will stay on the plant

for a couple of years, so it is worth looking after the plant to keep it tidy.

PROPAGATION

Fascicularia can be propagated by division, but this is quite a mammoth task. The individual rosettes with a little bit of root should be potted up and kept on the dry side while the roots establish. Alternatively, you can propagate by seed, which should be

The leaves of Fascicularia pitcairniifolia, *one of the few hardy Bromeliads, explode into red in late summer and early autumn.*

~

sown on the top of the compost, and it will germinate at a temperature of 13-15°C (55-60°F). This takes about two months and the seedlings are very small, so the young plants need to be grown on in a pot for some years before they are ready to plant out. In fact, it could be as long as five to six years before they first produce a rosette of flowers.

OTHER VARIETIES

F. bicolor H & S: 0.25 x 1m (10 x 36in). It is similar in style to *F. pitcairniifolia*, having the same clump-forming habit, but its leaves are dark green, thick and fleshy, and rather waxy to the touch. Established plants will form lots of rosettes, giving quite a spiky appearance and they will flower in late summer, producing between 20 to 40 small pinky-purple flowers in a head. It is not quite as tough as *F. pitcairniifolia*, but it should do well in a favourable location, although it could benefit from a covering of horitcultural fleece in the worst of the winter months.

Puya berteroniana

This wonderful plant makes quite an impact in the garden when it flowers, reaching a height of around 4.5m (13½ft) and a spread of 1.25m (4ft). It is also a member of the Bromeliad family and is native to central South America and, in the case of *Puya berteroniana*, particularly central Chile. It is used to growing in mountainous, desert conditions where the conditions are dry and there is little moisture, except perhaps for melting snows or rolling mists. So, it can do well in our more northerly climates, provided it is kept dry. It will tolerate temperatures of -5°C (23°F).

  P. berteroniana has long, arching, grey-green leaves (see page 65), usually 1m (3ft) in length, with marginal 1-cm (¼-inch) long spines that are hooked at the ends. These leaves form rosettes which send forth a flower spike of 2m (6ft). It flowers in high summer, producing large blooms with 5-cm- (2-in)-long, blue-green petals. The puya will not flower every year, but in favourable locations, usually on the coast, it will produce large clumps of rosettes that may send up flower spikes every second year or so. Many of the other plants in this chapter provide good complements to it, especially the yucca (see page 71) or agave (see page 66),

but it will also look good amongst some of the hardier grasses, such as the grey-leaved *Festuca glauca*, as well as sempervivum and sedum.

CULTIVATION

Site Selection In common with the other Bromeliads in this chapter, the puya really loves plenty of sun and dry conditions, either up against a wall with an overhanging roof providing shelter or amongst rocks in a rock garden or raised bed. It is possible to grow the puya in a container so that it can be taken indoors during the winter months to protect it, but bear in mind that it can get quite heavy and care should be taken when moving it.

Soil Again, the watchword is drainage, so if you need to replace the soil in the planting area, you should aim for a mixture of a soil-based compost, such as John Innes No. 2, and at least 50 per cent grit or sharp sand. This mixture can also be used for container-grown specimens.

Planting Puya planted outside should be put in their positions in late spring. Plant them at the same depth as they were in their pots. Avoid putting them in too deeply, or they will suffocate and rot. If you are growing puya in a container, do note that they doesn't like being potted on too often. Only pot them on to the next size up, don't jump to a large pot with a small plant. The rosettes of leaves will trail over the sides and look really attractive.

AFTERCARE

Feeding Puya need very little feeding. Only occasionally is it necessary to give these plants a small amount of liquid feed in the growing season.

Pruning Cut off dead leaves at the base, but be careful of the spines of nearby leaves attacking you as you do this! Like those of the ochagavia, the tips of the leaves tend to turn brown during the winter and it is a matter of personal choice as to whether you trim them off or not.

Winter Protection It is best to wrap these plants in horticultural fleece during the winter and, if possible, to put a glass frame over them to protect them from the worst of the rain. Container-grown specimens can be moved into a cool greenhouse until the spring.

Pests & Diseases Puya can get a bit of brown leaf-spotting, in which case it is a good idea to spray them with a systemic fungicide in the autumn in order to clean them up for the winter. Plants will then usually grow out of the problem as spring arrives. Mealy bug can prove a nuisance for container-grown specimens. For more information see page 19.

PROPAGATION

Mature puya usually form one big clump, but they can throw off a few smaller rosettes around their bases which can be broken off and potted up. This can often happen with container-grown plants. By far the best method of propagation, though, is seed, which should be sown on the surface of the compost and kept at a temperature of 13-15°C (55-60°F). It will take about two months to germinate. Young plants are very small in their initial stages, and it can be some years before they are large enough to flower.

OTHER VARIETIES

P. raimondii H & S: 3 x 2m (9 x 6ft). This species is very handsome. Its flowers are yellowy-green in colour and the grey-green leaves are 1-2m (3-6ft) long and about 6cm (2½in) wide. It is more delicate than *P. berteroniana*, tolerating temperatures of -4°C (25°F) for short periods.

MORE DESERT PLANTS TO TRY

Beschorneria yuccoïdes H & S: 2 x 1m (6 x 3ft). Resembling a yucca this striking plant has long narrow, blue-green leaves which sometime curl over at the tips. Each rosette of leaves only flowers once when it produces a large, arching spike up to 2m (6ft) high, which is rosy red and has nodding yellow-green flowers amid fleshy red bracts. It is hardy down to -5°C (23°F).

Chamaerops humilis (European Fan Palm) H & S: 2 x 1.5m (6 x 5ft). Europe's only native palm tree, it usually grows into a multi-headed clump of fan-shaped leaves which can be 80cm (32in) long and which flutter in strong breezes adding further interest to their strong shape. Golden-yellow flowers are produced on mature plants during summer and it is hardy down to -10°C (14°F).

Dyckia forsteriana H & S: 60 x 50cm (24 x 20in). This attractive South American Bromeliad forms a dense rosette of narrow grey-green leaves edged with recurved spines. Its flowers are small, numerous and pendulous with orange petals. An unusual plant that can be grown outside for most of the year, it will tolerate temperatures as low as -3°C (27°F).

Furcraea longaeva H & S: 1.5 x 1.5m (5 x 5ft). A handsome, vigorous plant resembling an agave, it has long, narrow, fleshy leaves which form a dense rosette. A flower spike is produced after many years reaching a height of 5m (15ft) with numerous small, pendant green-yellow flowers followed by young plantlets that are also produced on the spike. Only suitable for the mildest localities, it hardy down to -3°C (27°F).

Nolina longifolia H & S: 1.25 x 2m (4 x 6ft). This elegant rosette-forming plant has long narrow leaves which can reach 1m (3ft) in length. They are rough to touch and grey-green in colour. Hardy down to between -5°C (23°F) and -10°C (14°F), it rarely produces flowers, but if it does they appear in summer in a crowded panicle and are creamy white and flushed with pink.

Sedum dendroïdeum H & S: 30 x 40cm (12 x 16in). A delightful evergreen perennial, with succulent, apple-green leaves and stems, that is hardy down to -5°C (23°F), it originates from Mexico. Its small, flat-headed yellow flowers rarely appear.

Shady Places

$\sim$

Many gardeners, especially those who have just started gardening, tend to neglect shady sites, finding them unsuitable for growing many of the more brightly coloured flowering plants like those in the first section. But they are ideal for a whole range of delightful and attractive plants which may actually dislike the sun's heat. Indeed, the entries in the following chapters again share common features, but this time it is their love of moist fertile soils and dappled light of varying strengths as well as ample water in summer which will ensure luxuriant growth and handsome foliage.

The first chapter in this section concentrates on moisture-loving plants, while the last two chapters offer suggestions for varying positions in delicate shade or slightly denser woodland areas. Originating from quite diverse parts of the world, such as China, Tasmania, the high Himalayas and the forests of Europe and North America, the selection here offers you a variety of lush, verdant plants, such as the broad buckler fern, *Dryopteris dilatata*, or the majestic white plumes of *Smilacina racemosa*, together with shrubs like the attractive *Hoheria glabrata* with its numerous white saucer-shaped flowers. Whatever you choose, you may be certain that those corners you once ignored will become beautiful features from now on.

$\sim$

The moisture-retentive soil of this shaded border provides an ideal home for the prolific Rheum palmatum *(page 91), centre left in front of the hedge, and the fern* Dryopteris dilatata *(page 89), centre.*

Moisture-loving Plants

~

As you might expect, most of the plants in this chapter originate from habitats such as the banks of rivers and streams or rock faces and other embankments where there is water seepage. All these locations have one thing in common and that is a year-round supply of moisture. Some of these plants even grow with their roots permanently in water. They come from all around the world: South America, North America, South Africa, Europe and Asia. Many grow in full sun, while others prefer dappled shade.

As the constant supply of moisture is such an important factor in their lives, these plants can quickly wilt and suffer if that supply is interrupted. The varying light requirements are also important – the giant gunnera, for example, does best in full light where its leaves can reach huge proportions, while the dryopteris fern can also grow in full light so long as it does not get too hot and is not subjected to drying winds, but ideally it prefers some shade.

Those plants that usually live by rivers and streams often grow in soil deposited by floods. This alluvial soil is high in nutrients and one of the most fertile there is. So for the best results these plants should be planted in a soil that is as rich.

SITE SELECTION

It may seem obvious, but the wettest part of the garden is the best for these plants. Water travels downhill, so a depression or a lower part of the garden will usually be more moist than the surrounding area. Avoid areas that get hot during summer because they will require frequent watering. Pool-side locations are good, provided that the pool has an overflow. Don't assume that the soil next to your pool will always be moist; some of the driest areas in my garden are next to the pool because it is lined with concrete and so no water seeps through. The same applies to butyl and fibreglass liners and other pre-formed plastic pools.

What I have done is to cut out a piece of capilliary matting and place one end of it in the pool and bury the other in the soil. Water then travels up the matting and into the soil, so keeping it moist. You can buy capilliary matting at any good garden centre.

If your soil is generally dry, try planting at the side of your house which receives the most wet weather. You can also consider redirecting the drainpipes from the roof on to the planting area as well. This can make a lot of difference during the summer when a heavy shower will result in a substantial amount of water running off an average roof.

SOIL

It can't be stressed too much that the plants in this chapter need a soil which holds moisture and which doesn't dry out easily. Adding lots of organic matter will improve its water-holding capacity but, if your soil is very free-draining and prone to drying out, there are two options:

1 You can place a non-permeable membrane under the top soil which will prevent the water from draining away and will create boggy conditions for the plants. Doing this is a lot of hard work, but it gives you the opportunity to enrich the soil at the same time.

2 You can add one of the new water-holding polymers to the soil. These are frequently sold for hanging baskets and tubs and they absorb many times their own volume in water and can be added to garden soil. It can be a bit expensive, but you can use the polymer at a local level, just in the vicinity of the plant, and mix it with any available organic matter.

WINTER PROTECTION

In very cold areas plants like the gunnera and the zantedeschia may require some simple winter protection, but generally these plants are hardy. For further details on winter protection see the chapter on tender plants, page 23.

Gunnera manicata

(GIANT RHUBARB)

As the largest foliage plant that can be grown outside in Britain, *Gunnera manicata* presents an amazing spectacle with its prickly edged leaves that can reach a diameter of 2.5m (8ft), and with a general height of about 2.75m (9ft) and an overall spread of 4m (12ft) it needs a lot of room. But if you have the space, you really should try growing it.

Despite its common name, the gunnera is not related to the rhubarb at all. In fact the name refers to the size and shape of the leaves and it actually originates from southern Brazil and Colombia. During the summer this perennial produces flower spikes of about 1m (3ft) in height which have quite a primeval quality to them and which produce thousands of small greeny-brown flowers on small spikes.

Fairly frost-hardy, the gunnera will withstand temperatures between -10°C and -15°C (14-5°F).

It looks very good planted next to water at the edge of a pond or stream, and I think it is put to best effect when it is on its own, but some people like to plant it with bamboos or with the skunk cabbage, *Lysichiton americanus* (see page 84), for a luxurious jungle feel.

CULTIVATION

Site Selection *Gunnera manicata* really needs a moist position and you should bear in mind its eventual size when you are choosing where to put it. With good light, you will get stronger growth and bigger leaves, but avoid positions that become hot during summer, or the foliage will scorch and the gunnera will look ugly. Avoid windy locations too, since although the leaves are tough, they can be damaged and torn by strong winds which makes them look ugly.

The best place is one that is slightly sheltered, possibly by neighbouring shrubs and trees, though, don't plant the gunnera in deep shade.

Soil Naturally occurring along river banks and in marshy places, gunnera like fertile soils which don't dry out. A deep fertile loam is best with lots of organic matter. However, they will grow in clay, sandy or peaty soils, provided they have lots of organic matter added and the soil remains moist. Clay soils are useful because they usually have high levels of nutrients to start with. My gunnera is in a clay soil and it receives a very heavy mulch of well-rotted manure each year which it enjoys.

Planting This is usually done in the spring. Plants are normally bought as potted-up seedlings or offsets from mature plants. Both should be planted as soon as possible. Water the gunnera in well and continue to water them until they are fully established. If you buy them when they are dormant, be careful not to cover the dormant bud with soil when you plant it. The bud should sit on the surface of the soil, since it is from here that the new growth will appear.

AFTERCARE

Feeding With all those huge leaves, gunnera like a nutrient-rich soil. If the soil is poor, you will get small leaves and unhealthy-looking plants. Give the gunnera a mulch at least once a year with some well-rotted manure, or use an organic fertilizer, such as bonemeal, but don't apply it directly to the roots as it will burn them.

Pruning Gunnera need little pruning with perhaps only the removal of the occasional damaged leaf. You can do this during the growing season as long as the plant has a constant supply of moisture and nutrients so that it continues to send up fresh growth. Cut the leaves off at the end of autumn and either take them away or use them as a mulch.

Winter Protection Although they are generally quite hardy, it is important that the dormant crowns do not freeze solid during winter. They can be easily protected with a mulch of straw or bracken, but I find it best to cut the leaves off during October, turn them upside down over the crowns and tie the leaf stalks together. The results look a bit like miniature tents, but they can be attractive if they are done well. Doing this deflects a lot of the winter rain away from the crown and shields it from hard frosts. If necessary, you can add extra protection by putting straw over the crowns before you place the leaves over them.

Pests & Diseases Gunnera are relatively trouble free, but occasionally they get the odd fungal leaf spot. This is usually insignificant and they are more likely to be damaged by sun scorch.

PROPAGATION

Large plants can be divided at the end of the dormant season, normally in early spring. They should be replanted as soon as possible after division to prevent the roots from drying out. You can also raise large amounts of plants from seed which is best sown fresh when it becomes available during autumn. Sow it on a sandy mix and keep it at a temperature of 16°C (61°F). Some seedlings will germinate quickly while others will follow in the spring. When they are large enough to handle, pot them up into 7-cm (3-in) pots in a potting compost such as John Innes No. 2. These plants can then be grown on until they can be transferred to 15-cm (6-in) pots. They can then be overwintered in the pots in a sheltered location before being planted out in their final positions in the spring.

OTHER VARIETIES

G. tinctoria H & S: 1.5 x 1.5m (5 x 5ft). Similar to *G. manicata*, it has a shorter rhizome and more compact foliage which usually reaches about 60-150cm (2-5ft) in diameter. It produces a shorter flower spike of about 70cm (28in) with reddish brown flowers. *G. tinctoria* is a native of Chile and likes the same conditions and treatment as *G. manicata*. *G. prorepens* H & S: 10 x 45cm (4 x 18in). It is better for a small garden. A native of New Zealand, it has purplish-red leaves which are 3cm (1½in) long and red berried fruits of about 10cm (4in) in diameter.

Lysichiton americanus

(SKUNK CABBAGE)

This robust herbaceous perennial is mainly grown for its unusual looking bright yellow flowers which appear during spring. *Lysichiton americanus* grows to 40cm (16in) high and makes a lovely spectacle in the garden. It is the leaves of this

~

Gunnera manicata *looks good when planted with ligularia, particularly* Ligularia przewalskii *(page 86) shown blooming, inset.*

The optimum position for the spring-flowering Lysichiton americanus *is at the side of a pool or stream and it looks spectacular when reflected in water.*

~

native of western North America which give the plant its common name and which are often overlooked. A beautiful fresh green with a delicate bloom, they emit a musky odour. After flowering, the leaves develop, reaching a length of about 50-125cm (20-60in) and a width of 30-80cm (12-32in).

Lysichiton grow mainly in moist woods and at the sides of streams and they are at their happiest when growing in constantly wet conditions either in full sun or shade. Fully hardy, it can withstand temperatures of -15°C (5°F). With its strong shape, the lysichiton looks good when planted on its own by a pool or with other pool-side plants, such as *Iris pseudacorus* (yellow flag iris) and the candelabra primulas, *Primula japonica* and *P. pulverulenta*.

CULTIVATION

Site Selection Lysichiton need a location that won't dry out and grow at their best if they are kept permanently wet. So a pool-side or stream-side location is best. If the pool is made of concrete or plastic (both are impermeable), try planting the lysichiton where the pool overflow is. Alternatively, choose a low-lying area of the garden where water collects. They don't mind full sun or dappled shade and they will grow successfully under deciduous trees. This is because they develop early in the year and so complete a lot of their growth before the trees are in full leaf.

Soil These plants prefer a rich, fertile soil, but they will grow in clay and sandy soils which have had lots of organic matter added to them. The organic matter helps to conserve moisture in the soils and it can also be used as a mulch for the lysichiton or you can choose leaf mould, bark or garden shreddings.

Planting Planting is normally done in late spring when the lysichiton are showing signs of growth. If the plants are the result of division, it is important that they have adequate roots, otherwise they can die. The best thing is to plant young plants that have been raised from seed. Whichever you try, water them in well after planting. If the soil is prone to drying out, you could consider laying down an impermeable membrane (see page 82).

This can be laid in the soil at a depth of about 30-45cm (12-18in). Use a tough-grade polythene which will prevent the water from draining away and create a mini bog garden in the immediate vicinity.

AFTERCARE

Feeding Lysichiton will benefit from the occasional dressing of bonemeal

Pruning As they are herbaceous, the only pruning required is the cutting down of dead foliage in autumn. But take care not to cut through the growing bud when doing this.

Winter Protection Lysichiton are hardy and so do not need any protection in winter.

Pests & Diseases Aphids may attack young foliage but this is rare.

PROPAGATION

This is usually done by seed which should be sown as soon as it is ripe or purchased. Sow the seed and just cover it with seed compost. Stand the pot in a tray of clean water to keep it saturated. Seedlings may appear in the autumn or, more usually, the following spring. These can be potted up into 7-cm (3-in) pots when big enough to handle and grown on as necessary.

Planting out is normally done two to three years after germination and plants may take a further five years to flower. Established plants will flower most years from then on. When dividing plants, ensure that the minimum root disturbance takes place, otherwise they frequently die when transplanted.

OTHER VARIETIES

L. camtschatcensis H & S: 40 x 60cm (16 x 24in). Smaller in habit, its flowers are white and it looks very attractive when grown with *L. americanus*. Hybrids of the two will arise when they are grown near one another.

Ligularia przewalskii

A strong-growing herbaceous perennial, the beautiful *Ligularia przewaskii* is a native of northern China. Reaching a height and spread of about 1.25-2m (4-6ft) x 1m (3ft), it makes quite a splash with its tall purple-stemmed flower spikes that can get as high as 2m (6ft) and which produce hundreds of daisy-like yellow flowers in mid to late summer.

It is fully hardy and, given its origin, can withstand temperatures down to -15°C (5°F).

Ligularia tend to form a dense clump and look very good in large drifts when the flower spikes are set off by the dark green, deeply cut, round leaves and when planted with other moisture-lving plants such as hosta, hemerocallis (day lilies) and *Matteuccia struthiopteris* (Shuttlecock fern); (see page 104).

CULTIVATION

Site Selection Ligularia flower best when they are in an open position in full light. They will tolerate some shade, but may be shy to flower or not flower as well. They are, however, useful for planting in lightly shaded areas because their foliage makes excellent ground cover. Ligularia are really at home at the side of a pool or stream. And while they don't like to sit in water, they do need a constantly moist soil to prevent them from wilting during the summer. They also need to be sheltered from strong winds which can snap off the tall flower spikes. So, planting in the middle or back of a border will ensure that they get some shelter from surrounding plants.

Soil Ligularia need a constant supply of water. A deep, fertile loam with plenty of organic matter therefore suits them best. They will happily grow in other soils, but may not reach their full size, especially if the soil is prone to drying out. It is possible to grow ligularia as woodland plants in dappled shade provided the soil is moist.

Planting Dormant crowns can be planted at any time between mid autumn and early spring, as long as the soil is not frozen. Before planting, make sure you add plenty of organic matter to the soil, like well-rotted manure or leaf mould, and that it is thoroughly incoporated. This will help retain the moisture in the summer.

You can buy ligularia plants during the growing season and, if you do so always try and select a non-flowering one because it will establish quicker. Plant them as soon as you can as they don't do well if kept in their pots. Water the plants until they are thoroughly established.

AFTERCARE

Feeding Ligularia appreciate some well-rotted manure forked into the surface of the soil in which they are to grow and as a mulch. Alternatively, you can apply a dressing of bonemeal in spring, but don't put it directly on to the crowns. Or you can add a slow-release fertilizer to the soil at planting time.

Pruning Since ligularia are herbaceous they need very little pruning, apart from the annual cutting down of dead foliage during the autumn.

Winter Protection These plants don't need protection from the cold. But be careful that any stream or pool-side position will not become waterlogged as the result of winter rains.

Pests & Diseases Generally trouble-free, although aphids can infect young growth in the spring.

PROPAGATION

Ligularia are usually propagated by dividing established plants. This is normally done either in late winter or early spring. You can also propagate by seed which should be sown in the autumn in a standard seed compost and kept in a cold frame. Germination will take place place the following spring.

OTHER VARIETIES

L. stenocephala H & S: 2 x 0.60m (6 x 2ft). It produces yellow-orange flowers on a flower spike of 1.25m (4ft) and its foliage is less deeply cut than that of *L. przewalskii*. *L. dentata* 'Desdemona' H & S: 1.25 x 0.60m (4 x 2ft). It has very dramatic leaves that are dark purple on the top and mahogany underneath. It produces deep orange flowers.

Zantedeschia aethiopica
(CALLA LILY, ARUM LILY)

Even the smallest of gardens should allow space for this most beautiful of moisture-loving plants. Well-grown examples can reach a height of 1.25m (4ft) and a spread of 60cm (2ft) with heart-shaped leaves of 40 x 20cm (16 x 8in). Its fresh, light green foliage is produced throughout the growing season and tall flower spikes appear all through the summer bearing single 12-23-cm- (5-9-in)-long, white flowers (spathes). It is not uncommon for plants to flower up until the first frosts and the flowers look at their best when set off against the glossy green leaves of well-grown plants. Hardy down to -7°C (19°F) and even -10°C (14°F) for short periods, *Zantedeschia aethiopica* will tolerate lower temperatures if the crown is planted under water.

This species looks at its best when planted with other moisture-loving plants such as *Iris pseudacorus*, hosta and *Pontederia cordata*. Alternatively, it can be planted as a single specimen in a large pot or barrel and stood in either a pool or a tray of water when it should be placed in a prominent place.

CULTIVATION

Site Selection Zantedeschia appreciate a warm position, but they are equally at home in full sun or partial shade. Plants in deep shade are unlikely to flower on a regular basis. In their native South Africa they are found by stream sides and in wetlands. If the plants are to be left outside all year, choose a warm west- or southwest-facing position.

Soil It is very important that the soil has sufficient organic matter. Zantedeschia like a rich loam-based soil high in organic matter. In areas where the soil is a free-draining and sandy one, it may be necessary to place the plants in a pool, otherwise they will dry out constantly. Heavy clay soils can be improved a lot with the addition of organic matter.

The smooth sculpted flowers of Zantedeschia aethiopica *make a stylish display in the summer, adding an elegant touch to a sheltered corner.*

~

Planting This is normally done during late spring when the soil has had time to warm up. Plants are usually obtained as dormant tubers or as young plants in full growth. The latter can be planted straight into the garden after the fear of frosts has passed. When planting into a pool, never plunge the plants in at their final depth; support them on bricks and gradually lower them down over a period of weeks. This acclimatization process is very important, otherwise plants may die.

If you get dormant tubers, pot them up in a compost such as John Innes No. 2 and water them sparingly until the first shoots appear. Then increase the watering as the plants develop. When they are in full growth, they can be watered freely.

AFTERCARE

Feeding Plants grown in pots need a weekly feed of liquid fertilizer through the growing season and plants in pools can benefit from a couple of aquatic fertilizer tablets (sold for water lilies) added at the beginning of the season. Don't feed during the winter months unless the zantedeschia are in full growth under glass.

Pruning Plants need frequent tidying up. Cut off dead or damaged leaves, taking care not to cut through the young shoot inside. When cutting plants down during the autumn, take off only the damaged foliage and do not cut them down hard. If you do, you will damage any young shoots inside and allow the frost to penetrate.

Winter Protection In cold areas plants will need insulating with a mulch of chopped straw or bracken, garden compost, leaf mould or shredded bark. Plants grown in pools should be low enough in the water so that crowns do not freeze. A minimum depth of 15cm (6in) is usually enough, but plants can be planted in up to 1m (3ft) of water. If the pool freezes over in winter, the crowns will be protected underneath the ice.

Zantedeschia grown in pots can be taken indoors to a cool greenhouse or conservatory for the winter.

Pests & Diseases Zantedeschia can suffer from various diseases. Tubers are prone to rot from a bacterial soft rot and the fungus phytothora will also kill roots and cause brown streaks on the leaves and flowers. And the leaf spot fungus, *Phyllosticta richardiae*, causes grey-black blotches on the leaves, leaf stalk and flowers. Cucumber mosaic virus shows up as irregular streaking on the foliage and tomato-spotted wilt virus causes white spots and streaks on the foliage and stem blotches. Virus-infected plants must be destroyed and replaced. The control of sap-sucking insects like aphids is also important in combating viruses. Fungal spots can be treated with a systemic fungicide.

PROPAGATION

Zantedeschia can be grown easily from seed which should be sown fresh whenever possible. Seed which has been allowed to dry can be pre-soaked in warm water for 24 hours before sowing. It will germinate quickly at 21-27°C (70-80°F). Plants grown from seed will normally flower in their third or fourth year. Alternatively, plants can be divided up when they are coming into growth. Divisions can be potted or replanted immediately.

OTHER VARIETIES

Z. rehmannii H & S: 80 x 7cm (32 x 3in). It has thinner leaves than *Z. aethiopica* and a smaller flower that is suffused with pink. It will only tolerate temperatures of 7-10°C (40-50°F) and above. *Z. albomaculata* H & S: 1.25 x 0.60m (4 x 2ft). This has long, ivory, white, cream or occasionally pink flowers whose bases are blotched purple inside and foliage that is streaked with transluscent markings. It is only hardy to 10-13°C (50-55°F), but is worth experimenting with outside.

Dryopteris dilatata

(BROAD BUCKLER FERN)

The buckler ferns are a large group all requiring similar conditions. They are found as far apart as North America and Asia. Some species are native to Britain, like *Dryopteris dilatata*, which can be found in woods, hedged banks and shaded places.

It is fully hardy, deciduous and ideal for planting in a shady border or woodland garden (see page 80). When fully grown it reaches a height of 1m (3ft) and a spread of 1.25m (4ft) and each leaf or frond can be as much as 1m (3ft) long and 40cm (16in) wide, although they are usually slightly smaller.

Its foliage is delicate and a lovely fresh green. In shaded places it will arch out to capture the light, producing a very graceful effect. This can be used to advantage if it is planted in a raised bank or dry stone wall backed with earth, where the foliage will be fully appreciated.

D. dilatata looks most attractive when planted with other ferns, like the shuttlecock fern, *Matteuccia struthiopteris* (see page 104) and the royal fern, *Osmunda regalis*. It can also be used to good effect when planted with other shade-loving plants like hellebore, primula and pulmonaria.

CULTIVATION

Site Selection Dryopteris will grow in full sun, but they do best in dappled shade where the fronds will not get burnt by strong sunlight. In deep shade they grow more slowly and can be slow to establish. They also prefer a humid environment, so avoid planting them where hot, dry winds will scorch the foliage.

Plant them under shrubs, or on the shady north or east side of the house. This type of area can be difficult to get many plants established in, but it's just the sort of spot that ferns like.

Soil Most species, including this one, are tolerant of a variety of acidic and alkaline soils (pH 4.5-7). The soil must never become waterlogged, but remain moist.

Some species prefer a totally organic soil-less compost made up of dead leaf litter, while others prefer a loam-based soil. In general, though, a well-drained loam-based soil with plenty of organic matter will be suitable. If you are adding organic matter, don't use manures as these are too strong. Leaf mould is the best material, but chopped or shredded bark can also be used.

Planting Planting is normally done in the spring. When planting it is very important not to cover the crown of the fern, otherwise it will rot. Add plenty of leaf mould or composted bark to the soil. This will improve its moisture-holding capacity and provide the right growing environment for the fern roots. Plants must be watered in well and you should continue watering until they are established. Once they are, dryopteris can prove to be remarkably drought-tolerant.

AFTERCARE

Feeding In general, ferns don't like too rich a soil and so require little or no feeding. If your soil is poor, you could add a natural composted fertilizer. But use it sparingly.

Pruning Damaged fronds can be removed as required. They should be cut down cleanly to the base of the crown without leaving a long stalk. Remove any dying fronds during autumn.

Winter Protection Being fully hardy, dryopteris don't need frost protection. However, it is always advisable to mulch ferns in the autumn after they have been tidied up to ensure their roots are protected from frost. It is also easier and safer to mulch in autumn rather than spring when new delicate growth is beginning to emerge.

Pests & Diseases Generally trouble-free, but the fronds can play host to a rust which leaves brown spots, though it rarely disfigures them.

PROPAGATION

Ferns are usually propagated by spores (not seeds). These can be collected from the spore cases on the undersides of the fronds from midsummer to early autumn. They should be sown immediately or the following spring (I prefer to wait until the spring). Don't cover them with compost, but with a piece of glass. Place them in a well-lit position, away from direct sunlight, and never let the compost dry out. After several weeks a green growth will appear on the surface. This is the young ferns (prothallus). It's important at this point to keep the ferns moist, but water from below because the young plants are very delicate. In a couple of months small fronds will start to appear and when these are large enough to handle they can be potted up into 7-cm (3-in) pots. It's easier to prick out a group of ferns rather than an individual one. After two growing seasons, the ferns should be large enough to plant in their final positions.

Mature plants can be divided during spring, but they take some considerable time to settle down afterwards. After division and replanting they should be shaded until they are fully established.

OTHER VARIETIES

D. affinis cristata (Crested Wood Fern) H & S: 45 x 50cm (18 x 20in). Its arching fronds are pale green with leaf tips forked into a crest. It prefers a soil-less mixture of near-perfect leaf mould and can tolerate boggy wet conditions. Very hardy, it is ideal for the streamside or bog garden. *D. erythrosora* (Copper Shield Fern) H & S: 60 x 60cm (2 x 2ft). An evergreen, its fronds are bronze when young before turning green. It prefers a sheltered position with dappled shade in order to do well.

Rheum palmatum

(ORNAMENTAL RHUBARB)

One of the best ornamental herbaceous plants that there is, *Rheum palmatum* is originally from north-west China. It is a large plant reaching a height of 1.5m (5ft) and spreading to 2m (6ft) and it requires an open position in which to grow well (see page 80). Its leaves may reach 50-70cm (20-28in) long and 50-90cm (20-36in) wide. A tall flower spike of about 1.5-2.5m (5-8ft) appears in summer. This has many small deep red flowers which look quite dramatic. It is most effective when planted on its own as a specimen perennial or with other moisture-loving plants like *Zantedeschia aethiopica* (see page 87) and *Darmera peltata* (see page 92).

CULTIVATION

Site Selection Rheum do best in full sun in the open border with other herbaceous perennials, but they need shelter from strong winds. They can also be planted next to pools and streams, but it is worth remembering that the large foliage can easily shade a small pool completely. Their height and spread mean that they are more suitable for the back of the border where their full architectural shape can be appreciated.

Soil Rheum don't like waterlogged soil. Ideally it must have good drainage as well as being moisture-retentive and quite fertile which is most important if they are to produce sizeable leaves. I recommend a deep loam-based soil with lots of additional organic matter added. They will grow in clay, but this must be improved with organic matter. The soil must not dry out during summer as rheum wilt easily.

Planting Planting can be done any time from late autumn to early spring, providing the ground is not frozen. Pot-grown plants can be planted out during the growing season, but it is best to get these into the ground early on. When planting, mix some well-rotted manure into the hole. Don't plant directly into the manure. More manure can be applied as a mulch around the base of the plant to help suppress weeds and conserve moisture. Rheum have a large crown which should sit on the soil's surface, so be careful not to bury it when planting.

AFTERCARE

Feeding Fertile soil is important and extra fertilizer, such as bonemeal, can be mixed in with the soil at planting time. Alternatively, an annual mulch of well-rotted manure will ensure a steady supply of nutrients during the growing season. Extra feeds can be given in the form of a liquid manure.

Pruning Damaged leaves can be removed through the growing season and flower spikes should be cut down when the flowers have faded. In autumn the dead foliage should be removed: cut it down to the crown of the plant.

Winter Protection Rheum are fully hardy and require no frost protection. But losses can occur if plants sit in sodden ground.

Pests & Diseases Generally trouble-free, rheum can suffer from powdery mildew in dry weather when they are in need of water. This can be controlled with the application of a fungicide.

PROPAGATION

Plants may be divided in spring: lift crowns and cut them in two with a sharp knife or spade. These should then be replanted or potted up.

Some species can also be raised from seed which takes a while. It should be sown during the autumn and kept in a cold frame. Then the following summer the seedlings can be potted up and grown on ready for planting out in their final position during the spring after that.

OTHER VARIETIES

R. p. 'Atrosanguineum' H & S: 1.5 x 2m (5 x 6ft).
An excellent form with huge, deeply cut leaves of
1m (3ft) in length and 75cm (2½ft) wide which are
a deep red colour when they emerge, much of
which is kept on the undersides during the growing season. Flowers are produced in dense fluffy
panicles that resemble pampas grass in early summer
and are a vivid crimson. *R.
alexandrae* H & S: 1.25 x 1m
(4 x 3ft). Flowering to a
height of 1.5m (5ft), each
spike is covered with a lovely
cream-coloured bract which
is tinted red as it ages. It
really needs a cool, moist
position in order to grow
well.

Darmera peltata

A beautiful plant in every
respect, when it is fully
grown this hardy herbaceous
North American perennial
will reach a height of 1.25m
(4ft) and a spread of 1m
(3ft). Its large round leaves
are bright green and glossy
and are supported by strong
upright leaf stalks.

Mature *Darmera peltata* can
form dense clumps and are ideal
for stabilizing stream sides and
banks. Tall russet brown flower
spikes are produced well before the emerging leaves
in spring and they bear hundreds of small, pink
flowers, each with a red eye. In autumn the foliage
turns a beautiful reddish-brown before finally
dying down. It looks wonderful planted with *Gunnera manicata* (see page 83), hosta and hemerocallis.

CULTIVATION

Site Selection Darmera do very well by a pool or
in a bog garden, since they need ample moisture

The delicate pink flowers of
Darmera peltata *appear in spring*
well before the foliage emerges.

during the growing season, otherwise they can
tend to wilt on hot days.

They also like a well-lit position, but can tolerate some dappled shade. And if the situation is
very windy darmera will not reach their full size.
An open border or area of low-lying ground where
water collects would also be a good place.

Soil These plants should
have a moisture-retentive
loam with plenty of organic
matter in it. Darmera don't
mind some waterlogging,
but prefer not to grow in
water the whole time. Both
heavy and light soils need
lots of well-rotted garden
compost added to increase
their fertility and moisture-
holding capacity.

Planting This can be done
at any time during the dormant season up until the
spring. Potted plants can
sometimes be bought dur-
ing the growing season and
these should be planted as
soon as possible as darmera
demand a lot of water and
are unsuitable for growing in
containers. Each plant has a thick
rootstock which naturally sits on
the soil's surface, so refrain from
covering this when planting or it
may suffocate. Mulch new plants
with organic matter and do the same to mature
plants on an annual basis.

AFTERCARE

Feeding Established plants will benefit from a top
dressing of fertilizer in spring. If the plant is near
water, be careful not to spill the fertilizer into it. I
usually give a small dressing of a slow-release fertilizer to the soil when I'm putting in new plants to
give them a boost in their first year.

Pruning Damaged leaves can be cut off when necessary and all the foliage can be cut down at the end of the autumn.

Winter Protection In general this hardy herbaceous plant doesn't need any protection in winter.

Pests & Diseases Generally trouble-free.

PROPAGATION

Mature plants can be divided in autumn or later on in spring and can either be potted up or replanted in the garden. It's important when doing this to ensure that each piece of rhizome has a good growth bud on it when selecting small pieces for replanting.

Plants can easily be raised from seed too. This ripens in high summer and it can then be sown in early autumn. Or it can be sown early the following spring. It should hardly be covered by compost and the pots should be placed in a cold frame.

Germination normally takes place within eight weeks. When the plants are large enough to handle they can be potted up in to 7-cm (3-in) pots and grown on prior to a further repotting or being put out in their final position.

OTHER VARIETIES

D. peltata 'Nana' H & S: 30 x 40cm (12 x 16in). Well worth growing if you have a small garden and ideal for planting around a small pool. It has pink flowers and light green round leaves.

MORE MOISTURE-LOVING PLANTS TO TRY

Astelia nervosa H & S: 50 x 60cm (20 x 24in). Hardy down to -10°C (14°F), this striking plant has long narrow leaves covered in silver hairs and small, fragrant, greeny-purple flowers on a loose spike which appear in summer. It likes a moist, but not boggy, position in full sun.

Cautleya spicata H & S: 50 x 60cm (20 x 24in). This robust herbaceous plant has broad lanceolate foliage with red flower bracts and yellow flowers on an erect spike that appear in late summer. A member of the ginger family, it is hardy down to between -5°C (23°F) and -10°C (14°F) and likes a moist soil and a warm, sunny position.

Dierama pendulum (Angel's Fishing Rod) H & S: 2 x 1.5m (6 x 5ft). This perennial sends forth a

graceful, arching flower spike that is covered in bell-shaped, cerise-pink flowers in summer. Hardy down to -10°C (14°F), it prefers full sun and a moisture-retentive, but not waterlogged soil.

Impatiens tinctoria H & S: 2.10 x 1.5m (7 x 5ft). This delightful plant has light green foliage and succulent stems and produces large white flowers with a deep maroon throat in late summer through to autumn. Hardy down to -10°C (14°F), it likes a warm, sunny location and a moist, moderately fertile soil in summer.

Lobelia cardinalis (Cardinal Flower) H & S: 100 x 25cm (36 x 10in). A tall, striking perennial with purple-bronzed foliage and

bright red flowers which appear in summer, its narrow habit makes it ideal for growing up through other plants. Hardy down to -5°C (23°F), it thrives in a moist, sunny position and will tolerate being grown in water.

Thalia dealbata H & S: 2 x 1m (6 x 3ft). A beautiful marginal plant, it has broad, lanceolate grey-green leaves of about 40 x 20cm (16 x 8in). It produces a flower spike from between the tightly packed leaf stalks which is about 2m (6ft) in height and which bears small, violet purple flowers from summer through to autumn. A native of the southern United States and Mexico, it is hardy down to between -5°C (23°F) and -10°C (14°F), provided it is planted at least 20cm (8in) below the water's surface.

Delicate Shade-loving Plants

⁓

As the title suggests, the plants in this chapter require delicate shade in order to grow well. All the plants originate from the more temperate (i.e. milder) regions of the world, such as parts of North America, China and Tasmania. Most of them are found growing in or near forest or woodland areas.

People usually think of woodlands as being dark places, but often this is not the case. Generally, there will be clearings and glades among the trees where sunlight filters through the branches to the ground and, as a result, much of its harsh strength is subdued by the trees' leaves. So the plants growing beneath thrive in either dappled light or direct sunlight for part of the day. These conditions also provide a cool, deep root run which won't dry out during the summer months, but which give shelter from cold winters and drying summer winds.

At first glance, it might seem a bit difficult, not to mention expensive, to create a woodland glade in your garden, but it need not be. You can create the same conditions on a smaller scale, with just one plant. And, personally, I think if you have a small garden, it is best to grow a few plants well than to grow too many poorly.

SITE SELECTION

Delicate shade-loving plants will be at home underneath a tree or large shrub. If you have neither of these features, you can grow them in the open border provided they receive the shelter and partial shade that they need from surrounding plants. Do avoid any positions that are really hot and sunny, or dry – in other words the sort of places where the plants in the tender, hardy sun-loving or desert chapters would do best. The dappled shade of an old apple tree is ideal, but don't try growing plants under a tree like the beech as this casts too dense a shade and your plants won't flourish. In my garden, most of the delicate shade-loving plants grow under a *Magnolia* x *soulangeana* and this popular hybrid produces just the right amount of shade.

In a mixed border, try growing these plants amongst shrubs. If the shrubs don't have any overhanging branches, plant to one side where the sun will only reach for part of the day. If you plant on the north side of a shrub, you will ensure that your plant does not receive direct sun; planting on the west side will allow the plant sun in the later part of the day, and on the east side it will have sun in the morning. Avoid putting your plant on the south side of the shrub as this means it will get direct sunlight for most of the day and it will be too hot.

Usually the side of the house is a difficult area to grow plants, since it is often shady. Well, it can be the perfect site for these delicate shade-loving plants. The biggest problem you may find with this situation is the strong winds which can be funnelled down the side of houses. This can result in the plants' foliage being damaged or drying out during summer. If you have a problem like this, try growing a small hardy evergreen tree or shrub, such as *Viburnum rhytidophyllum*, to act as a windbreak.

SOIL

Delicate shade-loving plants come from many parts of the world and so grow in a wide range of soils. All these soils have one common characteristic: they are moisture-retentive at the same time as being free-draining. This may sound like a contradiction in terms, but 'good' soil can hold a large amount of water as well as having ample pore space which will contain small pockets of air that are vital for plant roots to grow.

In these plants' original environments the top soil is frequently made up of large amounts of organic matter (fallen leaves and other forms of dead vegetation), while the layer of soil beneath is free-draining and gritty. And a high rainfall means that the soil never dries out. The key to creating these conditions in your garden is well-rotted organic matter. Many books preach about the virtues of organic matter and with good reason.

It's the single most important thing you can add to the soil, because it holds it together and helps to create its structure. Maintaining this structure is essential for healthy root and plant growth. If your soil contains a lot of organic matter, it will dry out less during the summer and retain more moisture. For improving your soil see page 16.

PLANTING

Planting can be done at any time of the year, providing the soil is not too dry or frozen, but probably the best times are in the autumn and spring. At these times the soil is warm and moist and the plants can establish quickly. Avoid treading on the soil if it is too wet, as this will only damage that all-important soil structure. If the soil sticks easily to your boots and tools, then it's too wet and you should either wait for it to dry out or stand on boards raised above the level of the planting area.

Always put your plants in at the same depth as they were in their pots. If your plants have bare roots, put them in as quickly as possible, taking care to keep the roots covered while they are out of the ground. This will prevent them from drying out and dying.

Give the plants a shake as you plant them to help the soil fall in amongst the roots. It is important, but if the soil is too wet and sodden it can be difficult. Gently firm the plants into place, water them in and give them a mulch. I like to use an organic mulch, such as well-rotted manure, leaf mould or mushroom compost. This helps the soil as it breaks down and the worms take it in.

Alternatively, you can use a polythene sheet or woven plastic membrane, but these can be expensive, though they are very effective if your planting is to be permanent from the outset. However, if you decide your plant is in the wrong place or it has become too large, it can be difficult to lift and/or resite without damaging the mulch.

WINTER PROTECTION

Most of the plants in this chapter are hardy and so need no winter protection, but some like *Dicksonia antarctica* (tree fern) do. It can only tolerate a couple of degrees of frost for a very short time.

Polystichum setiferum

(SOFT SHIELD FERN)

One of the most attractive and versatile of evergreen ferns the soft shield fern has a graceful habit with leaves (fronds) reaching up to 1.25m (4ft) long, although 60cm (2ft) is more normal. These fronds arch out to give each plant a delicate shape (see page 96).

Each leaf blade is covered in dry, pale orange scales, which from a distance give the plant a rather woolly appearance. Fully hardy, *Polystichum setiferum* usually grows to 60-100cm (2-3ft) high and 60-125cm (2-4ft) wide.

It originates from southern, western and central Europe and looks very attractive when planted as a group under a shrub or tree. Alternatively polystichum can be planted with spring-flowering hellebore, primula and bulbs. It is hardy down to -30°C (-22°F).

CULTIVATION

Site Selection Polystichum prefers a cool, sheltered position away from drying winds. They can be grown in full light providing they have ample moisture, but really prefer dappled light. If they are grown in heavily shaded conditions, their growth will be much reduced. The north and east sides of buildings are ideal locations for planting. They like a well drained position, and in the wild they usually grow amongst rocks.

Soil These ferns prefer a soil that has a pH balance of 6.5-7.5 – in very acid soils they gradually loose vigour. A loam-based soil that is not too rich in nutrients suits them best. Grit can be added to improve the drainage and organic matter should also be incorporated to improve the soil structure. They dislike a constantly wet soil and excessive winter damp can cause problems with rotting.

Planting Planting out is normally done in spring and throughout the summer during moist spells. Don't cover the crowns with soil, water them in thoroughly and continue to water them until they have established.

AFTERCARE

Feeding Polystichum do not like a rich soil, but if they are planted in a general loam-based soil no additional fertilizer will be needed.

Pruning As polystichum are evergreen they do not really require cutting down during the autumn. New fronds will appear the following spring when you should cut down last year's fronds as they can harbour fungal diseases.

Winter Protection *P. setiferum* needs no winter protection, but some of the more tender varieties of this fern may. Fern fronds should be placed over the plants' crowns in early winter. These can be removed the following spring after the last frosts.

Pests & Diseases Generally pest-free, these ferns are prone to some fungal disease. *Taphrina wettsteiniana* is related to peach leaf curl. Its symptoms are black spots on the upper surface of the leaves and white layers of fruiting bodies on the undersides. Affected plants should be sprayed with a systemic fungicide during late winter and early spring. Heavy infections may need further sprays throughout the growing season.

PROPAGATION

Polystichum can be raised from spores (see 'Propagation' under '*Dryopteris*', page 90), but you can divide mature plants in spring by cutting them in half with a sharp knife and either repotting or planting them back in the border. In both cases they should be shaded until they have re-established themselves.

The feather-like foliage of Polystichum setiferum arches out to capture the diffused light.

~

OTHER VARIETIES

P. acrostichoides (Christmas Fern) H & S: 100 x 60cm (3 x 2ft). The Christmas fern is traditionally cut for seasonal decorations in its native North America. Its leaves are deep green above with hair-like scales below which are almost white on new fronds. It is easy to grow and fully hardy.

P. setiferum 'Divisilobum' H & S: 60 x 125cm (2 x 4ft). Its immense fronds arch out and lie flat in winter. Each side leaf tip is divided twice at the tip and three times lower down. This is also easy to grow and fully hardy.

Smilacina racemosa

(FALSE SOLOMON'S SEAL)

A superb plant both in and out of flower, this hardy herbaceous perennial produces strong growth each spring which will reach a height of 1m (3ft) and a similar width, though it will spread slowly. The leaves are small and oval and clasp the stem to the top, where plumes of creamy-white flowers appear in early summer and turn pink as they age (see page 101). If pollinated, these are followed by shiny, red berries in autumn.

Originating from the colder parts of North America, *Smilacina racemosa* is a tough plant – hardy down to -20°C (4°F) – that likes ample summer moisture, but if it is grown in full sun and the soil is allowed to become dry, then it will wilt and its foliage will brown at the edge. It is therefore best grown in dappled shade where the foliage will remain in peak condition.

Its glossy foliage is highlighted when it is planted with matt-leaved plants such as hosta and geranium. Equally it looks most attractive when planted with *Meconopsis bectonicifolia* (see page 123), *Dicentra spectabilis* and *Polygonatum x hybridum* (Solomon's Seal).

CULTIVATION

Site Selection A cool moist position in dappled or part shade is what smilacina like best. Choose a position under a tree that casts light shade. Alternatively plant near a shrub or fence that will cast shade for part of the day. Summer moisture is particularly important and soils must not be allowed to dry out. So choose a place in the garden where the soil is deep and remains moist.

Soil A deep fertile loam is best with plenty of added organic matter. Smilacina will grow in heavy clay and free-draining sands, both of which should have well-rotted organic matter added to help the drainage of one and the moisture-holding capacity of the other. Mulching is also very important to suppress weeds and conserve precious summer moisture.

Planting This can take place at any time during the dormant season, from the end of autumn to the beginning of spring. Where possible plants should have the root ball slightly broken up so that the outside roots can be spread out in the planting hole. Soil mixed with leaf mould can then be pushed in around the roots and firmed gently. This should ensure that plants will settle in quickly.

Potted plants can be planted when dormant or in growth, and these should be thoroughly watered in until fully established. Mulch all new plantings with organic matter and do not disturb them for a few years after planting.

AFTERCARE

Feeding Smilacina are not gross feeders but they will do better where there are adequate nutrients in the soil. It's therefore essential to maintain soil fertility by adding organic matter.

New plants will benefit from some fertilizer added into the planting hole. I think a slow-release fertilizer is best.

Pruning Very little pruning is required, apart from the removal of damaged stems and the cutting down at the end of the autumn of the top shoot growth.

Winter Protection Smilacina are hardy and so require no protection against winter cold, but in frost pockets young emerging growth may need light frost protection in early spring.

Pests & Diseases Slugs and snails may damage young shoots and leaves.

PROPAGATION

Vegetative propagation is done by division during the dormant season. Clumps can be broken down into small pieces providing they all have a shoot tip or dormant bud. These can either be potted into a loam-based compost, such as John Innes No. 2, or planted back out in the garden. Seed can be collected from the plants in autumn. It is advisable to collect this as soon as it ripens otherwise it will be lost to the birds. Seed can be sown in autumn or early spring and placed outside in a cold frame where it should remain cool.

OTHER VARIETIES

S. stellata (Star-flowered Lily of the Valley) H & S: 50 x 50cm (20 x 20in). Similar to *S. racemosa,* it has leaves of 15cm (6in) in length which are lanceolate and pale green. The flowers are small, with up to 20 borne on short stalks, crowded together on a terminal raceme 7-10cm (3-4in) long, and white to white-green. They appear in early summer.

Aralia elata 'Variegata'

(JAPANESE ANGELICA TREE)

This lovely east Asian deciduous shrub has an upright habit, forming thickets of slender, seldom branched stems which can reach 4m (12ft) high. Established plants can form small colonies as much as 3m (10ft) in width and these look really dramatic when planted in an open lawn or as a clump in a woodland garden. Tolerating temperatures between -5°C (23°F) and -10°C (14°F), *Aralia elata* 'Variegata' is only found in cultivation. It has margined leaflets blotched creamy-white which turn silver-white as they age, and numerous small, creamy-white flowers cluster together on spikes up to 40cm (16in) long, making an attractive cloudy sight in summer (see page 101). Often they are followed by small purple-black berries which contrast well with the yellow autumn colour of the foliage.

Aralia look their best when planted as specimen plants. In small gardens it may only be possible to plant one, but where space allows a group can look good. Their delicate outline can be appreciated when they are on their own in grass or an island bed. Alternatively they should be grouped with smaller plants such as *Tellima grandiflora* 'Rubra' (see opposite), *Hemerocallis flava, Geranium* 'Johnsons's Blue' and *Rodgersia podophylla*.

CULTIVATION

Site Selection Being hardy, aralia tolerate most situations in the garden, providing the soil does not become waterlogged or dry out completely. They do best in delicate shade, particularly the variegated forms, as strong sunlight soon damages the new foliage. Drying winds can also cause problems with leaf burn, so avoid putting plants up against south-facing walls or in sun traps. If you cannot provide dappled shade, then choose a position that only receives sun for part of the day. The north and east sides of buildings provide good positions, but plants in a north-facing site may be slower-growing if planted in permanent shade.

Soil These plants need a well-drained yet moisture-retentive soil. They dislike heavy sodden clay and free-draining sandy soils can dry out quickly in droughts. Soils should be improved with the addition of well-rotted organic matter. I prefer to use either leaf mould or composted bark chippings. Compost could be used, but avoid farmyard manure as this is often too strong and can lead to excessive luxuriant growth which is prone to winter damage.

Planting Planting is best done in the spring when new plants will grow quickly. Potted plants can be planted at any time during the growing season.

Ensure that they are well watered in and do not dry out. Apply an organic mulch of bark, compost or leaf mould to new plants.

AFTERCARE

Feeding Aralia don't need a lot of feeding. Plants grown in shallow soils over chalk may show signs of lime-induced chlorosis which can be rectified by the application of a sequestrated iron solution. It works very quickly, but in the long term a frequent mulch of well-rotted organic matter will produce a more acceptable rooting zone.

Pruning Very little pruning is required for aralia. Occasionally stems that have flowered heavily lose their growing tips and will have to be cut back to a lateral bud. These are not always easy to see and it is often better to wait until they start to shoot before pruning. Dead wood may occur from time to time and this should also be removed.

Winter Protection No winter protection is needed normally, although in very cold areas potted plants will benefit from being brought in under cover. This is particularly important for the variegated forms. Good drainage is vital when cultivating aralia in pots as winter wet can cause problems with rotting.

Pests & Diseases Generally trouble-free, but watch out when buying plants that have been grown under glass as these can often have red spider mite.

PROPAGATION

All aralia except variegated forms can be propagated from seed, which is best sown fresh in autumn and put outside in a cold frame. Germination will normally take place only after a period of stratification of 3-4 months at 4°C (39°F). Alternatively, large shrubs can be lifted and divided in later winter or early spring. Plantlets can be cut off and either potted up or planted out. Portions of stems can be cut off and potted up, but make sure that each has at least one visible bud on it. Young shoots will eventually appear from the dormant stem.

All variegated forms are produced by grafting

onto a stock plant that is of a green form. Variegated forms do not do so well on their own roots and taking cuttings is a waste of good material that could be cut up smaller and used for budding or grafting. After grafting on to a pot-grown stock plant, the plant is best put into a heated closed case where the level of humidity should be kept high. This will help to prevent drying out and encourage a rapid fusion of the two portions of tissue.

OTHER VARIETIES

Aralia elata H & S: 4 x 3m (12 x 10ft). The hardier parent plant which also has creamy-white flowers on spikes up to 60cm (2ft) long. *Aralia elata* 'Aureo-variegata' H & S: 1.5 x 1m (5 x 3ft). It has wide leaflets with irregular yellow margins.

Tellima grandiflora 'Rubra'

(FRINGE CUPS)

A very useful hardy, semi-evergreen plant, which makes ideal ground cover, *Tellima grandiflora* 'Rubra' is equally at home in sun or shade, but is at its most attractive when grown in delicate shade. There the foliage does not become burnt during hot summer months, and in a shaded area – where the soil does not dry out completely – its foliage will remain fresh and handsome. It is fully hardy, withstanding temperatures as low as -15°C (5°F).

A woodland plant from western North America, it will form individual clumps reaching a spread of 60cm (2ft) and when flowering the stems can get as high as 60cm (2ft). Flowering occurs in early summer on tall slender spikes when many small, creamy, pendulous flowers appear which are fringed with pink as they age (see page 101). The foliage is tinted bronze especially after cold weather or in bright sunlight, but underneath the leaf remains more or less green. Because of their non-invasive qualities they make excellent ground cover plants, ideal for the rockery, woodland garden, border or container. They look most attractive when planted with other woodland plants like primula, bulbs, orchids and the Himalayan poppy, *Meconopsis betonicifolia* (see page 123).

CULTIVATION

Site Selection Tellima like delicate shade so I normally plant them under shrubs or within the shade of trees and walls, and I've seen them put to good use in containers as filling plants where the main subject might be an ornamental shrub or tree. I like to plant them around herbaceous plants in the winter and early spring when the border can look a bit bare and the tellima provide some shape and colour.

Soil They prefer a humus-rich soil with plenty of well-rotted organic matter added to it, I use leaf mould because this forms a soil similar to the one they originated in. They dislike heavy wet clay soils. If you have this soil type, then either remove and replace a small area where you intend to grow the tellima or improve it (see page 16).

Planting This can be done at any time of year. Pot-grown plants can be planted throughout the growing season. You should make sure that the soil used to backfill the hole is broken up well and has had some organic matter added. Water plants in well and if necessary remove some of the foliage to prevent them wilting.

AFTERCARE

Feeding Providing the soil has a reasonable level of nutrients to start with, additional feeding is not really needed. In poor soils plants may require a spring dressing of a slow-release fertilizer. This can either be an inorganic resin-coated bead type or a more organic one, such as bonemeal.

Pruning Very little pruning is required except the removal of the dead flower spikes. Plants may also need some cutting down at the end of autumn.

Winter Protection This is seldom needed but, being semi-evergreen, plants may get damaged during very cold and windy spells. This is not normally a problem and they will produce new growth in the spring.

Pests and Diseases On soft young growth aphids can be a problem in spring and early summer on developing flower spikes. Vine weevil can be a threat to established plants. Make sure when buying plants that they are healthy and vigorous; a plant that is wilting in moist soil almost certainly has root problems which could mean vine weevil infection. Plants near lawns may get eaten by cutworm, and these should be removed and destroyed.

PROPAGATION

Established plants can be lifted and split at any time during the dormant season when weather permits. Even young plants grown in pots can sometimes be split when they are planted out. Only a very small piece of stem is needed to grow a new plant. Tellima have very fragile roots and care should be taken when lifting established plants or most of the root will be lost. Tellima grow quickly from seed which should be sown in a cold frame during the autumn. Germination normally takes place the following spring. Purple-leaved forms do not come true from seed. If you don't want to collect seed from the flower spikes, make sure they are cut down after the flowers have faded, to ensure that all the energy goes back into the plant.

OTHER VARIETIES

T. grandiflora 'Perky' H & S: 45 x 60cm (18 x 24in). It is ideal for a small garden with small rounded leaves and red flowers in summer. *T. grandiflora* 'Pupurteppich' H & S: 60 x 40cm (24 x 16in). Its foliage is an attractive burgundy colour in summer. The flowers are borne on dark stems and are large, green and fringed with pink. This is an extremely attractive form and well worth growing.

Veratrum album

(FALSE HELLEBORE)

A superb plant in every respect, primarily grown for its foliage and form, it also produces a dramatic flower spike in early summer. This herbaceous perennial from Europe, North Africa and Asia reaches a height of 1-1.25m (3-4ft) each year and produces a profusion of strong shoots when established. Its flowers are small and white outside and

green inside. Many hundreds of them are produced on a single branched spike.

Veratrum album has extremely handsome foliage, especially when young. Strong shoots appear in spring and as these open the corrugated surface of the leaves can be seen (see page 105). This foliage can only be maintained in peak condition if the plant is grown in dappled shade and has a constant supply of moisture throughout the summer. Plants grown in strong sunlight soon go yellow and the foliage browns at the edge. If starved of water, plants wilt quickly and growth is much reduced.

V. album is hardy, tolerating temperatures as low as -15°C (5°F) and it looks excellent in the woodland border with similar moisture-loving plants like meconopsis (see page 121), hosta, hellebore, pulmonaria and anemone.

CULTIVATION

Site Selection Veratrum need a constant supply of moisture and dappled shade throughout the summer in order to grow well. A position in the garden that does not get too hot suits them best. Avoid sun traps and choose an area that perhaps receives sun only for part of the day. Alternatively plant under a tree or in a clearing in amongst shrubs.

Soil A deep, fertile, moisture-retentive soil is best for these mountain plants. Plenty of organic matter should be added to the soil and around the plants as a mulch. Large amounts of organic matter might have to be added in areas where the soil is thin and free-draining. However, although summer moisture is important, soils must not be badly drained or prone to waterlogging.

Planting Dormant plants can be lifted and moved during autumn and during spring just as growth is beginning to start. Potted plants can be planted at any time of year, but when plants are purchased in

~

The white plumed flowers of Smilacina racemosa *(page 96) are complemented by the interesting foliage of* Aralia elata *'Variegata' (page 97) and the fragile spikes of* Tellima grandiflora *'Rubra' (page 99).*

the spring it is best to get them into their permanent positions as soon as possible as veratrum do not like being kept in pots.

Care should be taken with the swollen roots which break easily. Make sure they are spread out gently in the planting hole before it is back filled. When planting, add plenty of well-rotted organic matter to the soil used to backfill the hole and put some in the bottom of the hole as well.

Newly planted veratrum should be well watered in and mulched with organic matter. I like to use leaf mould as this mimics the plants' natural environment. Alternatively, farmyard manures can be used providing that they well-rotted.

AFTERCARE

Feeding Veratrum appreciate a fertile soil and the fertility can be increased by the application of some organic matter, like leaf mould. Or you could use an organic slow-release fertilizer such as bonemeal or an inorganic one, such as a resin-coated slow-release fertilizer.

Pruning Very little pruning is required except the removal of dead foliage and stems at the end of the autumn and the removal of dead flower spikes.

Winter Protection This is not normally needed, but in very cold districts, where late frost may be a problem, young emerging shoots can be covered with a layer of leaf mould, straw or bracken to prevent damage.

Pests & Diseases Generally trouble-free except for slugs which can cause problems in spring and early summer on new growth.

PROPAGATION

Plants can be lifted and divided during the autumn and spring. I prefer to do this in the spring when growth is beginning to start. A split crown should be replanted or potted immediately. Plants produced at this time settle in slightly quicker, though it may be a couple of years before they have really established and start to produce large handsome foliage again.

Seed should be sown when it is fresh as old seed that has been allowed to become dry will almost certainly be dead. This is best done in the autumn and it should be put in a cold frame.

Seed needs a period of stratification, (about three months) at a temperature of 1.6-4.4°C (35-40°F). This should be followed by a period of warmth at 21°C (70°F). Seedlings produce a small leaf in their first year and only start to grow adult foliage in their second. Plants cannot be expected to flower for the first three or four years.

OTHER VARIETIES

V. nigrum H & S: 1.25 x 1m (4 x 3ft). Flowers are purple-black and appear in summer. They are borne in large numbers on a tall spike 30-100cm (1-3ft) high. *V. viride* H & S: 125 x 40cm (48 x 16in). It has long leaves of about 30cm (1ft). A native of Northern America, its yellow-green flowers are produced during summer on a tall spike. This species is very hardy and has hairy foliage when young.

Jeffersonia diphylla

(TWIN LEAF, RHEUMATISM ROOT)

A delicate little plant originating from the woodlands of eastern North America, *Jeffersonia diphylla* is a hardy herbaceous perennial which reaches a height of 30cm (1ft) when fully grown.

Leaves of 15cm (6in) across are grey-green below and have a waxy bloom above which repels water (see page 105). Delicate flowers appear in spring with the new leaves and are a papery white and about 2.5cm (1in) across. This little plant forms a clump when mature, which will seldom exceed a spread of 20cm (8in). But groups of plants can be placed together to form large carpets of colour in the spring.

A hardy plant, the jeffersonia will tolerate a temperature of -15°C (5°F), it prefers the dappled shade of the woodland and is most at home when planted with other small woodland plants like viola, anemone, primula, pulmonaria and the pretty blue-flowered *Corydalis flexuosa*.

CULTIVATION

Site Selection Dappled shade suits jeffersonia best, so choose a site that does not get direct sun. I've planted mine in two spots, one at the base of a north wall, the other under a hosta.

When the hosta is in full growth the jeffersonia is dying down and of course the jeffersonia is in full growth when the hosta is just shooting through the ground. They can also be successfully planted underneath shrubs and trees. Try not to choose a spot that gets too dark too early in the season, i.e. a tree species that comes into leaf early and casts a dense shade, like a horse chestnut.

Soil The soil needs to be high in organic matter. In their native home jeffersonia are usually found growing in woodlands over limestone, so don't plant them in an acidic soil. They are happy in both neutral and alkaline soil. Jeffersonia usually die down by midsummer and so moisture-retention in the soil is only important for them during the spring and early summer.

Planting Jeffersonia can be planted in autumn or spring, whereas potted plants can be planted when in full growth. Make sure that they are given enough water at planting time and if possible apply an organic mulch, like leaf mould or bark chippings. Once plants have been planted in their final positions they are best left for several years before splitting. Established and undisturbed plants will flower more reliably.

AFTERCARE

Feeding Providing the soil is reasonably fertile there will be no need to apply additional fertilizer. Normally the annual application of leaf mould or bark chippings will continue to add sufficient nutrients to the soil.

Pruning Plants are usually cut down in high summer when the foliage has begun to die. Other than this no pruning is required. Remove seed heads once the flowers have faded if you are not planning to raise jeffersonia from seed, so that this energy goes into the vegetative growth of the plant.

Winter Protection None needed.

Pests & Diseases Jeffersonia are generally trouble-free.

PROPAGATION

Mature plants can be divided during the autumn and spring although it is easier to see the plants in the spring as they come into growth. These should be replanted immediately. Divisions can be made on small plants as long as there is a growth bud present on each of the new plantlets. To ensure a clean cut use a sharp knife. Jeffersonia seed will take up to 18 months to germinate. It is best sown as soon as it is ripe in trays of seed compost and put either in a cold frame or cool greenhouse. After germination leave the seedlings in the tray for another year they can then be potted up into 7-cm (3-in) pots and grown on. Plants raised from seed may take up to five years to flower.

OTHER VARIETIES

J. dubia H & S: 30 x 20cm (12 x 8in). The young foliage emerges a purple-violet colour and then fades to pale violet. The flowers appear before the foliage and are a pale lavender colour. It is an ideal plant for the peat garden or ericaceous bed and, like *J. diphylla,* it appreciates a high level of organic matter in the soil.

Podophyllum hexandrum

An interesting plant deserving more popularity. Originating in the hills and mountains of western China, *Podophyllum hexandrum* has long been used in traditional Chinese medicine, although it's worth mentioning that the leaves and seeds are poisonous. This hardy little woodland plant tolerates temperatures of -10°C (14°F) and is at its best in spring and early summer when the foliage is still fresh and when it is in flower. Reaching a height of 30cm (12in) and a spread of 40cm (16in) when mature, *P. hexandrum* is a herbaceous perennial which produces strong new growth each spring. Leaves up to 25cm (10in) across are held above the ground on rigid stalks. As the new foliage emerges in spring it reclines backwards at an angle of 45°. Eventually, as it matures, it lifts up and is held horizontal. New foliage is a deep bronze colour with green veins and this colour remains with the foliage throughout the year, only fading slightly as the foliage ages (see opposite). White-tinged pink, papery flowers appear in spring sitting just above the foliage. These open up in sunlight and show the golden-yellow stamens within and they are followed by shining red fruits.

Being woodland plants podophyllum are best planted with plants requiring similar conditions, like *Polygonatum odoratum, Convallaria majalis, Helleborus foetidus, Dicentra formosa* and *Asarum canadense*. These will all grow successfully together and look good in a combined planting.

CULTIVATION

Site Selection Podophyllum appeciate dappled or part-shade. Plants placed in deep shade are unlikely to flower, but in half-shade will do so each year. If they are planted in full sun, the foliage loses its quality during summer and the leaves soon scorch. Summer moisture is very important if plants are to grow well and not be forced into an early dormant period. Choose a position where the soil is reasonably deep and fertile. As for many of the plants in this chapter, a position under some shrubs or within the shade of a tree is ideal. Avoid sun traps and also places that are prone to waterlogging.

Soil A fertile, moisture-retentive soil is best. Add plenty of organic matter, but avoid using peat as this will only acidify the soil and is a waste of natural resources. The best material is garden compost with leaf mould as a mulch.

Planting This is normally done in early spring before the plants are in full growth. Potted plants can be planted throughout the growing season, but it's best to get them into the soil to prevent them from drying out during the summer months. Plants must be mulched, either with the indispensable leaf mould or bark chippings or an organic mulch, such as coir or garden shreddings.

AFTERCARE

Feeding Generally podophyllum require little additional feeding if ample organic matter is applied on a regular basis, i.e. mulch each spring.

Pruning Each autumn the dying leaves should be cut down to ground level.

Winter Protection None needed.

Pests & Diseases Slugs and snails can cause damage during the spring and early summer. As the main attraction of podophyllum is the decorative foliage it is very important to keep an eye out for these garden pests, especially when rain has fallen at the end of a dry spell.

PROPAGATION

Plants can be lifted and divided in early spring and should be planted immediately.

You can also raise podophyllum from seed which can either be sown fresh or in the following spring. Seed trays containing a sandy free-draining seed compost should be placed in a cold frame and kept moist until germination occurs. Seedlings should be potted when they are large enough to handle and grown on for a season before planting out in their final positions.

OTHER VARIETIES

P. peltatum (Wild Mandrake or May Apple) H & S: 30 x 40cm (12 x 16in). Its leaf can be much larger than that of *P. hexandrum* and is mottled brown. It has a white flower and its fruit ripens to a rosy red. It originates from a slightly drier environment than *P. hexandrum* and so can withstand shortages of water better.

Matteuccia struthiopteris

(OSTRICH FERN OR SHUTTLECOCK FERN)

A vigorous herbaceous perennial that is hardy down to -20°C (-4°F), *Matteucia struthiopteris* can be found as far apart as North America, Europe and eastern Asia. Strong new growths, which are

brown and tightly furled, appear each spring unravelling from the centre of the plant, giving it an architectural appearance. These finally uncurl into delicate, light green fronds which resemble the tail feathers of an ostrich – hence its common name (see page 108).

The fertile fronds which appear in summer contain the spores from which new plants will grow and these are released in winter and these fronds can be left on the plants for winter effect. Mature plants can reach a height of 1m (3ft) with a similar spread. Plants multiply naturally by underground rhizomes and a single plant can colonize a sizeable area over a period of several years quite easily.

The coarse, corrugated leaves of Veratrum album *(page 100), top, contrast well with the lower-growing* Jeffersonia diphylla *(page 102), centre, and the brown-marbled foliage of* Podophyllum hexandrum *(page 103), bottom, all of which make the perfect backdrop for the delicate bluebells.*

~

Matteuccia can look very handsome on their own, when planted in a group, or when planted in a waterside location with other moisture-loving plants such as *Iris pseudacorus, I. sibirica, Hosta sieboldiana* and the royal fern, *Osmunda regalis.*

CULTIVATION

Site Selection This handsome fern is very easy to grow provided it is planted out of full sun and in a soil that does not dry out during summer. Plants will survive periods of drought, but their foliage will quickly burn and shrivel in sun traps, though they normally regrow the following spring.

In deep shade plants will grow slowly, but in delicate shade growth can be vigorous and they can get quite large in one year. Their foliage will also remain in peak condition for longer. Choose a site that does not dry out during summer and receives either dappled or part-shade – under the shade of a tree or large shrub is best.

Soil A moisture-retentive soil is needed to keep this delightful plant in good condition. When planting under trees, consider whether the tree is surface-rooting, e.g. a beech. The soil surface here will dry out quickly and the plant will be difficult to establish.

Oak, apple, pear and cherry trees, for example, have deeper root systems and so take much of their moisture from lower down and therefore it is possible to establish plants underneath.

Organic matter is very important to fern culture and matteuccia are no exception. As it rots down in the soil it provides the right rooting environment and holds moisture during dry spells.

Matteuccia will grow on a wide range of soils including heavy clays and free-draining sands as long as ample amounts of well-rotted organic matter are added.

Planting Plants should be planted in the dormant season as long as the ground is not frozen. Potted plants can be planted throughout the growing season and must be watered in well.

When planting, remember that these plants will spread once established. If plenty of organic matter has been added, then this spreading will start very quickly, within the first season. So new plants should be planted 1-1.25cm (3-4ft) apart, otherwise they will be too crowded. When planting, add lots of well-rotted organic matter to the soil. And give the plant a heavy mulch to suppress weeds and retain soil moisture.

AFTERCARE

Feeding Additional feeding to ferns always has to be done carefully: it's easy to over do it and scorch both roots and foliage. But matteuccia will benefit from a very light dressing of bonemeal dusted into the planting hole and possibly a light liquid feed when they have been in the same position for many years. Liquid feeds must be diluted to half their recommended strength otherwise you could scorch the plant. Ample additions of organic matter will continue to give ferns a boost each spring.

Pruning Each autumn the dying fronds will have to be cut down. They should be cut cleanly to the base with a pair of sharp secateurs – don't be tempted to clip them with shears as this produces an untidy effect. The brown fertile fronds of mature plants which will be standing in the middle should be left; they will provide some winter interest whilst the fern is dormant.

Winter Protection These hardy plants do not need protection from the cold, but to ensure that they dos not freeze solid in very cold areas make sure that they have an ample mulch of organic matter around their crowns through the winter.

Pests & Diseases Generally trouble-free.

PROPAGATION

Matteuccia are propagated very easily by the division of established crowns. The underground runner can be lifted and either potted or planted in a new location. Late winter to early spring is the best time for doing this. Many new plantlets can be obtained from a single plant and in future years can be used to plant up a dramatic drift.

Plants can be raised from the spores. Cut fertile fronds from the plants just before they open and place them in a warm dry room. The spores will fall out in a couple of days and can then be sown on the surface of moist, soil-less compost, such as coir seed compost, and covered with either a sheet of glass or a propagation lid. Plants will begin to grow after about six months with small adult plants beginning to show after about nine months. When large enough to handle, they should be potted up into an organic compost of half chopped bark and half coir and grown on for one year before being planted out in their final positions the following season.

OTHER VARIETIES

M. orientalis H & S: 60 x 60cm (2 x 2ft). A Chinese species, its fronds tend to be more spreading than *M. struthiopteris*. Fertile fronds reach 30cm (1ft) in length and are green at first, turning to brown. Although uncommon in cultivation, it has proved to be more drought-tolerant than *M. struthiopteris*.

Dicksonia antarctica

(SOFT TREE FERN)

One of the most beautiful ferns there is, this giant comes from southeastern Australia and Tasmania (see page 109). In its native environment it grows in wooded valleys, mostly in shade but sometimes in brighter light, and always near water. Plants can experience snow in their natural evironment and are hardy down to -5°C (23°F) in cultivation.

Dicksonia antarctica is a very adaptable species which can be grown outside in more mild and shel-tered areas and under glass in both the cool and warm greenhouse in colder areas. In suitable areas mature plants, which are slow to grow, can reach a height and spread of 4m (12ft). In their natural home they can reach 10m (30ft). The trunks are thick, fibrous and composed of columns of roots which should be kept moist, especially during the summer months.

This most handsome of ferns can either be grown as a specimen plant in the garden or under glass, or, in mild areas, it can be grown in groups under the shade of trees. Where it is possible to grow these giants outside they lend themselves to waterside planting with other foliage giants like *Gunnera manicata* (see page 83), *Rodgersia podophylla* and *Lysichiton americanus*, (see page 84).

CULTIVATION

Site Selection Dicksonia prefer shade to full sun, whether they are planted out or placed outside in pots during the summer. Plants deteriorate above temperatures of 32°C (90°F), so a cool shaded position suits them best. In gardens where they thrive outside they are normally found in moist wooded valleys, where summer temperatures are less severe. Choose a position which is partly shaded and preferably away from drying winds. During the summer they require frequent water-ing, so either locate plants near to an outside tap or invest in a DIY irrigation kit to cut down on watering time. When grown under glass, plants in south-facing conservatories must either be stood outside during the summer or heavily shaded and damped down.

Soil Organic composts are best: chopped bark, leaf mould, sharp sand and coir mixtures work well. When planting outside, the incorporation of organic matter cannot be overemphasized. Dicksonia pro-duce large amounts of roots annually and these need an organic mix to grow into. Plants should not be put into a heavy clay soil unless it has been so heavily improved that it resembles an organic soil. Plants which are permanently outside should be dressed with a heavy mulch of organic matter annually in order to keep the roots cool and pre-vent drying out.

Planting Plant dicksonia outside after the fear of frost has passed; late spring is best. The planting hole should be thoroughly prepared with copious quantities of additional organic matter. You may want to incorporate a seep hose or some form of irrigation pipe as well. Plants should be planted to the same depth that they were in their pots and given a heavy mulch. All plants must be watered in well and should continue to be until established. From then on they will need their trunks watered on a daily basis in dry weather and if they are under glass. Watering can be reduced during the winter when demand drops off.

AFTERCARE

Feeding Plants are slow to grow, but growth can be increased by the application of a balanced liquid feed applied at fortnightly intervals throughout the growing season. This should not be given if the plants have been allowed to become dry. Plants also benefit from the application of seaweed-extract fertilizer which can also be applied as a liquid.

Pruning Very little pruning is required except the removal of damaged or dead fronds.

Winter Protection In cold areas plants will need to be brought indoors during the winter, but in mild districts they can be left outside. If cold weather threatens, the trunks should be insulated with bracken or straw held together with horticultural fleece. The fronds are normally lost in cold weather, but will regrow the following spring providing the crown of the fern has had adequate insulation. Dicksonia from the mountains of Tasmania are now available from forest plantations and are proving to have a much higher degree of cold-tolerance.

Pests & Diseases Generally trouble-free

PROPAGATION

Plants produce no offsets, so vegetative propagation is difficult, but they can be raised from spores providing these are sown as fresh as possible. Plants raised this way usually establish well.

OTHER VARIETIES

D. squarrosa H & S: 4 x 4m (12 x 12ft). The stem of this interesting species from New Zealand only reaches 10-15cm (4-6in) in width and is branched. Branches can be cut off mature plants and rooted in an open organic compost during the spring. It normally requires protection during the winter.

~

Opposite: Dicksonia antarctica *revels in the delicate shade cast by surrounding trees.*

Below: The luxuriant foliage of Matteuccia struthiopteris *(page 104) looks at its best when the sun shines through the beautiful green fronds.*

MORE DELICATE SHADE PLANTS TO TRY

Agapetes serpens H & S: 70 x 60cm (28 x 24in). An evergreen shrub with small, glossy leaves and bright red, pendulous flowers that have darker 'V' markings. It has round, white fruit tinged with purple. Hardy to -5°C (23°F), it likes a moist, humid environment and mustn't be allowed to dry out in summer.

Aristolochia macrophylla (Dutchman's Pipe) H & S: 5 x 6m (15 x 18ft). This robust, deciduous climber is hardy down to -10°C (14°F). It is best grown in a sheltered location away from strong winds which can damage the heart-shaped leaves that display the yellow-green or

~

brown siphon-shaped flowers to their best advantage.

Berberidopsis corallina (Coral Plant) H & S: 4 x 4m (12 x 12ft). A scandent, evergreen shrub which is hardy to between -5°C (23°F) and -10°C (14°F), this grows best in an open, sandy, loam-based soil that is neutral or slightly acidic. It produces pendulous, deep coral-red flowers in large numbers in late summer.

Desfontainia spinosa H & S: 2 x 1.5m (6 x 5ft). A spectacular evergreen shrub with glossy,

dark green, holly-like leaves that have sharp prickles. It has long, tubular, orange flowers that are tipped with yellow and appear in profusion in summer. Hardy down to -10°C (14°F), it prefers a neutral to slightly acidic soil and a sheltered location.

Lapageria rosea (Chilean Bell-flower) H & S: 3 x 2m (10 x 6ft). A beautiful evergreen climber from Chile, this plant detests strong sunlight and is hardy to -5°C (23°F). It forms a tangle of thick branches and produces long, fleshy, bright red-pink flowers in late summer and early autumn. It needs the shelter of a wall to grow well.

Woodland Plants

⁓

Woodland habitats once covered most of the British Isles and a lot of our hedgerow plants lived at the woodland's edge. Today, you can still see extensive communities of bluebells carpeting these areas in spring and plants like the trillium described in this chapter naturally grow in large drifts over the woodland floor in their native habitat. I usually grow them in small groups, but over a period of time they can spread providing they are given the right conditions. Other plants in this chapter, such as the Japanese acers, grow as understorey plants in deciduous woodland which covers the mountains of their native country. In fact many of our garden plants originate from woodlands all over the world, from as far away as China, the Himalayas, New Zealand and South and North America, as well as nearer home in Europe.

All these plants like constant conditions: abundant moisture, diffused light or shade, shelter from strong winds and drying air and very gentle fluctuations in temperature. Some plants in this chapter, such as *Embothrium coccineum,* grow naturally in open scrub, but because the climate here is much cooler than in their native home they grow best in an open woodland situation. Early-flowering plants, like bluebells and the trilliums, don't find shade a problem, since they complete their life cycle quickly at the beginning of the year and are beginning to die down by high summer when the trees are in full leaf. Bulbs like these can be very useful for naturalizing under trees where little else will grow.

SITE SELECTION

As with the delicate shade-loving plants, providing the ideal situation for woodland plants in most gardens is not easy. But you can find suitable places if you look around. A favourite of mine is planting underneath existing trees and shrubs and it's surprising how many plants you can squeeze under even the smallest of fruit trees. You can plant these woodland plants in the open border either under or in between shrubs and perennials, so that all the plants transpire together to keep the air moist and cool. Avoid areas near large expanses of paving, such as a driveway or patio, though, because the air that comes off these in summer can be very dry and will shrivel the delicate foliage on many woodland plants, particularly the Japanese acers.

Again, planting at the side of the house is an option, provided it is not too windy (see 'Site Selection' in 'Delicate Shade-loving Plants', page 94), because woodland plants prefer cool, moist sites and here they will receive direct sun for only part of the day, if at all. Acers and hydrangeas can thrive in this sort of position, but plants like the hoheria and embothrium appreciate a little more light and warmth, so a border backed by existing shrubs is a good idea. Or you could plant them against the west wall of the house where it is warm, but intercepts wet weather.

SOIL

Woodland plants prefer their soil to be cool, deep, slightly acidic and full of organic matter. And it is important that it is moisture-retentive, because if the soil does dry out during the growing season the plants will quickly deteriorate.

The level of acidity in the soil can make quite a difference to some of the plants. For example, the flowers of the Himalayan meconopsis will produce a better blue colour if the soil is slightly acidic.

Improving the soil for growing these plants is straightforward, even if yours is a heavy, uninspiring clay. Adding ogranic matter is vital. It can be put in when preparing the soil for planting, during planting itself and as a mulch. Any well-rotted organic matter will suffice, though leaf mould and bark chippings are very good and, apart from the fact that the plants adore it, it looks very attractive on the soil's surface. But you can use any garden compost, or rotted garden shreddings or well-rotted grass clippings mixed with garden compost. It all helps to retain moisture and as these continue to rot they produce humic acids which help stick the soil particles together and lower the pH.

PLANTING

You can plant woodland plants at any time of the year, though spring and autumn are the best. As with the delicate shade-loving plants, it is a good idea to add more organic matter when planting and to shake the plants slightly so that as much soil as possible gets between the roots. If the weather is dry, put some water in the hole prior to planting to ensure that there is adequate moisture and some fertilizer, such as bonemeal, when you backfill the planting hole. Don't add too much though because it can burn the roots. (A modest handful sprinkled over a square metre is a useful guide.) Water the plants in well and apply a mulch (see 'Planting' in 'Delicate Shade-loving Plants', page 95).

WINTER PROTECTION

Plants grown in woodland areas seldom need protection from the cold. The natural environment of the setting helps to protect the more tender species from cold winds. Some plants, such as the meconopsis which has very hairy leaves, can succumb to the ravages of excessive moisture and rot. If they are prone to rotting during winter, then try to cover the plants with a simple cloche to keep the worst of the wet off. I grow a number of woodland plants at the base of a north-facing wall where it is cool and shaded and during the winter I can easily lean a simple frame light against the wall to keep the foliage dry, although the roots, of course, don't dry out.

Acer griseum

(PAPER-BARK MAPLE)

Of all the trees suitable for a small garden, the maples must rank as some of the most popular. They are grown for their autumn colour, delicate shape and attractive bark, but if I had to choose one it would be the paperbark maple. It encompasses all the strong maple characteristics and is ideally suited to urban and country planting, being hardy down to -20°C (-4°F).

A native of western China, *Acer griseum* will reach 12m (36ft) when mature in a woodland environment. When grown in the open, it usually reaches a height of 7m (21ft) and forms a rounded crown of 6m (18ft) wide. Plants can take many years to mature, so very often they are grown as young specimens and require very little space.

In the autum the dark green foliage of *A. griseum* turns a vivid orange-scarlet and during winter its beautiful peeling, cinnamon bark will be much appreciated (see page 112). It can either be planted with other autumn-colouring plants like Japanese acer or *Euonymus sachalinensis* or underplanted with autumn-flowering bulbs, such as *Colchicum autumnale* and *Crocus speciosus*. Alternatively, it is equally at home as a specimen in a lawn or border. Plants can be trained into informal shapes in pots, but watering is very important during summer as they can easily suffer if they become dry.

CULTIVATION

Site Selection As woodland plants, acer appreciate dappled light, cool conditions and ample moisture, but if all these cannot be provided in one spot, then these versatile plants will grow in less than ideal conditions.

Don't plant them in strong sunlight or in a soil that frequently dries out, otherwise the foliage will quickly burn and deteriorate. Windy positions should also be avoided as the delicate foliage can soon be removed by strong winds and burnt by sea spray. Choose a position among exisiting shrubs, at the end of the border or within the shade of the north side of the house.

Soil Acer require a fertile, moisture-retentive soil that does not dry out during summer. They will not tolerate bad drainage and waterlogging and do best on soils that have a neutral to acidic pH level.

Too much emphasis cannot be placed on organic matter which should be added into the soil and used as a mulch. Bark, shredded compost, leaf mould and well-rotted farmyard manure can all be

Acer griseum is a stunning plant at any time of the year, but particularly during winter when the shallow light catches the glorious russet-coloured peeling bark.

~

be planted below soil level. All plants need to be staked securely to prevent wind rock and, if necessary, the delicate young trunks can be protected with a fine netting surround which should, if possible, extend 60cm (2ft) up the tree. It is important that the netting remains on the tree until it is established. It will prevent the bark being nibbled by rabbits and other wildlife in country areas and being used as a scratching post by cats in urban areas.

AFTERCARE

Feeding In general feeding is not normally required, but plants grown in pots will benefit from a

put to good use, although the latter should be used sparingly and should not come into direct contact with the roots.

Planting Acer can be planted from dormant bare rootstock at any time from autumn through to early spring. Potted plants also can be planted at any time of year, but during the growing season care must be taken that they are well watered. It is important that the young tree is planted to the same depth that it was in the pot, or nursery bed.

Beware that some acer may have been grafted: it is vital when planting these that the graft union should remain just above the soil surface and not

fortnightly feed during the growing season with a general liquid fertilizer. On poor soil some additional fertilizer can be provided in early spring as a light dressing. Use one of the slow-release types.

Pruning Very little pruning is required except for the removal of dead wood. Plants grown in pots many need to be kept in shape by cutting back to the nearest pair of buds at the desired size. Larger branches can be removed with a pruning saw if necessary. Avoid the large-scale lopping of branches as plants may take many years to get back into shape, if at all.

Winter Protection *A. griseum* is very hardy but strong cold winds cause some shoots to die back. Where temperatures are expected to fall below freezing for long periods of time, plants in pots should be protected to prevent them from freezing solid.

Pests & Diseases Plants are susceptible to a variety of fungal diseases: coral spot, which manifests itself in the form of pink pincushions, causes smaller branches to die, while honey fungus will kill plants rapidly. If your garden has this persistant fungal problem, it's not worth planting *A. griseum* unless you choose an area that is definitely free of it. Verticillium wilts can cause sudden withering of foliage and shoots and stems will die back. Affected parts can be cut down to healthy wood as soon as the first signs of infection are seen. Then spray or drench the tree with a systemic fungicide.

PROPAGATION

Acer are mainly propagated by seed, which should be sown fresh whenever possible. It's worth checking the viability of seed prior to sowing by cutting some of the seed open to see if there is an embryo present. *A. griseum* seed does not produce a lot of seedlings in any one batch of seeds. Dry seed should be soaked in warm water for 24-48 hours prior to sowing. Then it should be stratified in damp sand or compost for a period of no less than 60 days and not more than 100.

Softwood cuttings can be taken in summer and rooted

in a heated closed case. They will benefit from a hormonal root dip prior to insertion into the compost.

OTHER VARIETIES

A. palmatum (Japanese Maple) H & S: 2-5 x 3-4m (6-15 x 10-12ft). A small tree or large shrub when mature, its rounded habit makes it ideal for waterside planting or for isolated specimen positions where its full beauty can be appreciated. During autumn its foliage turns bright red, although some cultivars will turn deep orange and yellow as well.

Trillium grandiflorum

(BIRTHROOT, WAKE ROBIN)

A superb little spring-flowering plant that will in time spread itself into a carpet of plants, this hardy herbaceous perennial from eastern North America grows quickly in the spring, reaching a height of 30-45cm (12-18in) and a spread of 30cm (12in).

~

Trillium grandiflorum *will carpet the springtime woodland floor with its lovely ice-white flowers.*

The stems are topped with three sturdy leaves spreading to 30cm (12in). At the centre of these leaves a single white flower is produced (see page 113). When open, this flower can spread to 10cm (4in) across and it contains a deep yellow centre. Some flowers may have a tinge of pink to them. By high summer the foliage will begin to die off and by late summer it will have completely disappeared.

An excellent plant to establish under shrubs or trees in a woodland garden or border, it is hardy and will withstand temperatures of -10°C (14°F). It looks good when planted with other spring flowering plants such as *Narcissus cyclamineus, Helleborus orientalis, Anemone nemorosa* and primula.

CULTIVATION

Site Selection Because these woodland plants die down from high summer, care should be taken on where to plant them. A position where they can be left alone is best. Avoid areas where you change planting schemes biannually, otherwise you may dig up the dormant rhizomes by mistake. A position under some shrubs is best or at the back of the border where the trillium can flower and complete their life cycle before all the herbaceous plants grow up and obscure them. Where space is limited they can be grown in pots and brought into the house just before flowering, the blooms can then be enjoyed without them being damaged by rain. Strong sunlight or areas that get very hot should also be avoided, as the sun will burn foliage and force plants into an early dormancy.

Soil Trillium appreciate a high level of organic matter in the soil. They tolerate a wide range of soils, but dislike bad drainage and heavy clay. A soil with a neutral to slightly acidic pH is best, but *T. grandiflorum* will grow successfully in slightly alkaline conditions. Plants should be mulched with organic matter during the dormant period, preferably in the autumn. The best material for this is leaf mould, but bark chippings or garden compost will also suffice. If planted in soil that remains moist throughout the summer, then trillium can grow in full sunlight, if it is prone to drying out the plants should be planted in part-, dappled or full shade.

Planting Plants can be obtained in two forms: dormant and growing. Dormant rhizomes should be planted as soon as they are available, normally late summer to early autumn. Plant individual rhizomes 10-15cm (4-6in) deep in groups. Alternatively, plant potted plants either as they come into growth or when in full growth. Ensure that plenty of leaf mould is put into the hole prior to planting and that the plant is mulched with leaf mould as well. Water plants in. Once planted they can remain undisturbed for many years.

AFTERCARE

Feeding Providing the soil is of modest fertility trillium will require no additional feeding. They will obtain what nutrients they need from their annual mulching of leaf mould. Plants grown in pots may require a light liquid feed after flowering and should be repotted every couple of years.

Pruning Once plants have died down and the foliage has browned, the old growths can be cut off.

Winter Protection No winter protection is needed from the cold, but it is important to plant trillium at the correct depth and to give them a mulch so they do not completely freeze. In their native home they are covered with a protective layer of snow each winter.

Pests & Diseases Generally trouble-free, but watch out for slugs and snails which will feed on young shoots and flower buds.

PROPAGATION

Plants can be increased by the division of established clumps. This should be done soon as the foliage has died down and the new plants should be potted or replanted immediately. Seed should be sown fresh whenever possible. Sow into pots or seed trays in a John Innes seed mix with 50 per cent added leaf mould. Then put into a cool position, preferably a cold frame. Germination may be slow and can take from 18 months to three years. When plants have finally germinated, they can be potted just before they go dormant and grown on in 7-cm

(3-in) pots for a further two to three years. Plants may take five years to flower from seed.

OTHER VARIETIES

T. sessile H & S: 30 x 12cm (12 x 5in). Its foliage is slightly leathery and mottled in various shades of green and brown and the flowers are dark maroon. It contrasts well when planted with *T. grandiflorum*. The form 'Snow Queen' has white flowers instead of maroon. *T. erectum* H & S: 45 x 40cm (18 x 16in). Its flower is smaller than that of the other species, but is a dark maroon colour and appears in late spring. This is set off by the fresh green, veined leaves.

Embothrium coccineum

(CHILEAN FIRE TREE, FLAMEFLOWER)

An extremely attractive, large, evergreen shrub or small tree, *Embothrium coccineum* has proved quite hardy down to -15°C (5°F) and, given a sheltered environment away from drying winds, it has been know to withstand temperatures of -32°C (-26°F), but this is exceptional. It is one of the few members of the huge southern-hemisphere *Protea* family which can be reliably grown outside in northern temperate areas. It can reach 10m (30ft) high and spread to 5m (15ft).

The leaves are narrow and a dark matt green and although *E. coccineum* is an evergreen, severe winter weather may account for substantial leaf loss.

A large quantity of small orange flowers are produced in late spring (see page 116) which make a spectacular sight and flowering may continue sporadically throughout the growing season. Even very young plants, providing they are propagated from cuttings, will produce flowers at an early age. Embothrium look good with rhododendron and camellia.

CULTIVATION

Site Selection Shelter from cold drying winds is the most important point to consider when choosing a planting position for embothrium. If possible, plant in an open woodland situation, or between some existing shrubs. Greater protection can be achieved if some of these are evergreen. In cold areas embothrium can be grown against walls. A west-facing wall is best as this receives sunshine at the end of the day and so does not thaw quickly after frost like an east-facing one. It also does not get as hot as a south wall.

Soil Embothrium prefer a peaty acidic soil, but will grow in neutral soils. They dislike excessively alkaline conditions. Over-rich soils should also be avoided as these produce an abundance of soft growth which is more frost-tender. Although originating from open scrub areas, embothrium are mountain plants and so are frequently enveloped in mists and cloud, therefore soils should not be allowed to dry out during summer. Choose a well-drained moisture-retentive soil and add plenty of organic matter to it.

Planting Planting is normally done in the spring after the threat of frosts has passed. Prepare the soil and add plenty of organic matter, such as leaf mould or chopped bark, into the planting hole. Plant all new plants to the same depth they were in their pots and thoroughly mulch new plantings with leaf mould to a depth of 8cm (3in). Water in well afterwards.

AFTERCARE

Feeding Embothriums are generally undemanding as regards additional feeding. However, on soils that are slightly alkaline lime-induced chlorosis can appear each year. Either improve the acidity of the soil with lots of organic matter or apply a solution of sequestrated iron several times during the growing season. Potted plants benefit from a weekly feed of liquid fertilizer diluted to half-strength through the growing season.

Pruning This is generally done after flowering in early summer. If sucker growths are looking untidy, cut them off at an early stage to promote the formation of a trunk on the tree. Alternatively, plants being grown as shrubs will need to have their leading shoots cut back to promote bushier growth.

Plants in pots may need to be pruned to shape - this can be done throughout the growing season providing the plant is growing vigorously.

Winter Protection Young plants outside should be protected from winds with insulation, such as straw, bracken or horticultural fleece. Or you could build a small netted screen around the plant.

Correctly sited, large plants should not need any protection from winter cold, but if severe weather threatens, then try to cover as much foliage as possible with fleece or netting.

Pests & Diseases Generally trouble-free.

PROPAGATION

Terminal cuttings can be taken either from suckering growth during summer, or leaf-joint cuttings from the current season's growth during summer. These should be placed in a propagator with a closed lid that has some gentle bottom heat. Root cuttings can be taken in late winter or early spring and inserted into a cold frame. New plants are notoriously difficult to raise from cuttings, so you must persevere.

Seeds can be sown during early spring and should be put under glass at a temperature of 13-16°C (55-61°F). Young seedlings should be pricked out when they are large enough to handle into 7-cm (3-in) pots in either an ericaceous mix or a John Innes mix which has no added lime.

After being grown on for at least two years, preferably under glass, they can be put in their permanent positions.

Late spring sees Embothrium coccineum *burst into a profusion of small fiery orange flowers.*

~

OTHER VARIETIES

E. coccineum var. *lanceolatum* (sometimes sold as *E. lanceolatum*) H & S: 10 x 5m (30 x 15ft). It is the same as *E. coccineum* but has narrower leaves, and is reliably hardier. *E. coccineum* var. *lanceolatum* 'Norquinco Form' H & S: 10 x 5m (30 x 15ft). This also has narrower leaves that often fall in winter and bright scarlet flowers.

Cardiocrinum giganteum

(GIANT LILY)

This really is a spectacular plant. *Cardiocrinum giganteum* is related to the lily family, but unlike them it dies after flowering (i.e. it is monocarpic). Generally reaching a height and spread of 60cm (2ft) when flowering, it can produce a flower spike up to 4m (12ft) high with as many as 20 large trumpet blooms. These are white with tinges of green and maroon on the outside (see opposite). Each flower may be as long as 30cm (12in) and it has a very strong, sweet fragrance. Flowering may take between three and five years if the plant is grown from bulbils and five to seven years from seed.

Originating from the mountains of southwest China and northwest Burma, this giant grows in dense, moist forests up to altitudes of 3000m (10 000ft), where it's often enveloped in cloud and mist for days at a time. Though hardy down to -10°C (14°F), it must not be allowed to dry out during summer or sit in cold, constantly wet conditions in winter. It looks good by itself or with meconopsis (see page 121) and veratrum (see page 100).

CULTIVATION

Site Selection In order to do well cardiocrinum need woodland conditions with shelter from strong winds, both dry and cold, and dappled sunlight. It may be difficult to provide all of these conditions in the average garden, but most can be provided by planting them in amongst shrubs and small trees. When planting near a building, choose a west wall that will offer some protection from the coldest of weather and will get the most of summer rainfall. But beware of choosing places around a building that are prone to wind funnelling, otherwise flower spikes are likely to snap off in their prime.

Soil As woodland plants, cardiocrinum appreciate a cool, moist, neutral to acid soil that holds moisture but is not poorly drained. The soil must be fertile and nutrient-rich in order for them to grow well. I have grown them on clay, but this was only made possible because I added a lot of organic matter. Well-rotted manure was incorporated into the planting hole and the plants were mulched with leaf mould twice a year. Thin and sandy soils should be treated in the same way.

The monocarpic Cardiocrinum giganteum *is a Himalayan treasure that is well worth the wait until it flowers.*

Planting Mature bulbs should be planted in the autumn with the tip of their dormant crown just below the soil surface. Sometimes it is possible to buy potted plants in the growing season and these should be planted as soon as possible – they must not be allowed to dry out. If you want to ensure a continuous display of flowers each year then it will be necessary to plant bulbs of different ages at the same time. Before planting, the hole must have some organic matter incorporated into it as deeply as possible. Add more to the soil used for backfilling and tease it around the roots of the plant. Finally, top it off with a deep layer of leaf mould. Water all new plants in well and continue to water them during dry spells until they are fully established.

AFTERCARE

Feeding A dressing of bonemeal around plants in the spring is worthwhile. Young plants in pots can be given a liquid feed once a week through the growing season.

Pruning At the end of the season any dead growth should be cut back to near ground level.

Winter Protection Cardiocrinum should have a heavy mulch of leaf mould of about 10-15cm (4-6in) to prevent their roots from freezing. Young growth is often damaged by frost, so it is important to protect this by covering the shoots with some conifer branches or some dried leaves, perhaps off the top of last autumn's leaf heap. These can then be pulled to one side in spring after the threat of frosts has passed.

Pests & Diseases Generally trouble-free, although slugs and snails can be a problem for young growth emerging during the spring (see page 19).

PROPAGATION

Although plants that have flowered die, the flowered parent bulb may produce many small bulbs as offsets before dying. These can be lifted and either replanted and grown on or potted up. Plants developing from these will take three to five years to flower.

The best-quality plants and flowers are raised from seed, but these take up to seven years to flower. Seed should be sown as soon as possible, preferably fresh from the plant, or if not immediately it arrives. Fresh seed will germinate readily. Sow it in a free-draining seed compost and place it in a cold frame. Seedlings will germinate after periods of moist cold and so often appear in late winter. Beware of early slugs and enterprising mice which will feast on this crop of green shoots. Seedlings should be potted up when they are large enough to handle and grown on for three years before being planted out into their flowering positions.

OTHER VARIETIES

C. giganteum var. *yunnanense* H & S: 2 x 0.60m (6 x 2ft). It is slightly smaller than its related species with dark purple stems and its flowers are often tinted green, a rich red in the throat and open from the top of the spike downwards. They also hang horizontally compared with those of *C. giganteum* which hang down. *C. cathayanum* H & S: 150 x 40cm (60 x 16in). It comes from eastern and central China and has flowers that are 10-13cm (4-5½in) long and appear in groups of up to five at the top of the flower spike. They are an irregular funnel shape, fragrant, creamy-white and spotted with purple above.

Hoheria glabrata

(MOUNTAIN RIBBONWOOD)

Often thought of as a large shrub, *Hoheria glabrata* eventually grows to the size of a small tree, reaching a height of 6m (18ft) and a spread of 3m (10ft). Its upright narrow branches are very flexible and bend down at the tips with the weight of the white rose flowers that appear in summer (see page 17). These are pure ivory white and last for about two weeks, though they are easily damaged by rough weather.

Native to open woodland in New Zealand this hardy little evergreen tree – it will withstand temperatures of –10°C (14°F) – of the mallow family requires a warm sunny position in open woodland to do well. It makes an excellent backdrop for hydrangea (see oppsoite), aralia (see page 97) and abutilon. Or use the hoheria as a frame for climbers such as *Eccremocarpus scaber* (see page 17).

CULTIVATION

Site Selection A sheltered warm position suits hoheria best. They dislike heavy shade, preferring to have light shelter from the intensity of the summer heat. In smaller gardens plants can be successfully positioned up against a warm west wall or in a sheltered southwest-facing corner, or in the mixed border in a sunny position. Having some evergreen shrubs nearby will help to shield this tree from the cold weather.

Soil Hoheria like a free-draining soil which does not dry out during summer. Poor drainage will lead to poor root growth and eventual root fungal problems. Heavy soils should be improved (see page 16), particularly the drainage element. Soils should be thoroughly and deeply cultivated to break up any consolidation that may have occurred. Hoheria thrive in both acid and chalky soils.

Planting Young hoheria are usually purchased as potted plants and they should be planted out in late spring after the fear of frosts has passed and the soil has had time to warm up.

Thoroughly cultivate the soil as mentioned. It is a good idea to add some leaf mould to the soil used to fill the planting hole. Plants will need to be staked as they are prone to rocking in strong winds. A simple stake can be driven in on the windward side of the stem just before filling the planting hole. Water all new plants in well and mulch with an organic mulch such as bark chippings, compost or leaf mould.

AFTERCARE

Feeding Hoheria appreciate a fertile soil that is not too rich. Strong manures and fertilizers should not be added to the soil as these can burn sensitive

118

roots. Adding some bonemeal at planting time and as a dressing during the spring is worthwhile.

Pruning Light pruning is all that is required. This is done after flowering when plants can be pruned to shape. Avoid making large cuts and removing major limbs as this will affect the plants' performance. This is less of a problem with young vigorous plants.

Winter Protection Hoheria doesn't need much protection, but young plants can be covered with horticultural fleece until they are established.

Pests & Diseases Generally trouble-free, although new growth can sometimes become infected with aphids during early summer. Young plants grown under glass are prone to whitefly and this should be watched out for when buying new plants.

PROPAGATION

Semi-ripe cuttings can be taken from late summer to early autumn. These should be 6-10cm (4-6in) long and should be from the current season's growth. Insert them into a well-drained cutting compost and if possible place into a heated propagation case. Softwood cuttings can be taken in late spring and these should be placed into a closed case or pot with a polythene cover, otherwise wilting will quickly take place. If placed out of direct sunlight, they should root within six weeks. Seed can be sown in spring and should be placed in a cool greenhouse or a cold frame. If kept at 21°C (70°F), germination will also take place within six weeks.

OTHER VARIETIES

H. lyallii H & S: 6 x 3m (18 x 10ft). The leaves are very hairy when young, eventually turning a grey-green colour as they age. Flowers are produced later than those of *H. glabrata*, normally showing in mid-summer. In cold areas it makes an interesting wall shrub. *H. sexstylosa* H & S: 6 x 4m (18 x 12ft). It has masses of small white flowers in summer, and the leaves are light green and polished with light brown stems. One of the most hardy of the evergreen species, it can easily be pruned into an informal shape, making it ideal for small gardens.

Hydrangea aspera ssp. *sargentiana*

An excellent hardy deciduous shrub with exceptionally large and handsome hairy leaves feeling like velvet when young, *Hydrangea aspera* ssp. *sargentiana* is a native of western China. It will reach a height of 3m (10ft) when mature and can spread to 4m (12ft). When grown in shade, its growth tends to be upright and arching, but in more light it will form a dense thicket of shoots.

Its flowers are the first to appear of any hydrangea species, usually blooming by midsummer. These appear as great flattened heads of pink-purple blooms. Surrounding these are large, white, sterile flowers often thought of as bracts which turn pink as they age (see opposite).

This is an excellent plant for the woodland garden where it grows well with other shade-loving trees, like *Acer palmatum* and *A. japonicum*. It also grows well in more light providing it does not get too hot, and can look great with contrasting foliage like the bamboo *Chusquea culeou breviglumis* or *Mahonia lomariifolia*.

CULTIVATION

Site Selection A cool semi-shaded spot is what is needed for this woodland plant. Dappled shade is best, but handsome plants can also be grown in part shade. I've seen good plants grown on north walls where direct sun rarely falls. Plants grown in warm sunny positions are likely to have their foliage burnt during the summer, which makes even the most robust plants unsightly. Choose an area either under an exisiting tree or within the shade of a building. Alternatively, plant the hydrangea among shrubs or up against a north-, northwest- or north-east-facing fence.

Soil Hydrangea prefer an acidic, moisture-retentive soil which is high in organic matter. They dislike soils that dry out during the summer months and also dislike excessively alkaline soils. An acidic or neutral to slightly alkaline soil suits them best. Shallow and heavy clay soils should be improved with organic matter.

Planting Planting can be done either during the autumn or the spring. Plenty of organic matter, such as well-rotted farmyard manure, should be added to the soil beforehand. Either mulch with the same or use bark chippings or leaf mould. Plants should also be watered in well and continued to be watered until established.

AFTERCARE

Feeding Additional fertilizer can be applied as a dressing to plants in spring – this is especially important for plants grown in containers which will soon exhaust all the available nutrients in the compost. I prefer to use bonemeal applied lightly under the canopy of the shrub. Fork it in gently, taking care not to disturb any roots.

Pruning Flowered stems can be removed during the autumn, but I like to keep them on the shrub for winter decoration. They can then be cut back the following spring to a healthy pair of buds. If the shrub has become overcrowded with thin shoots, remove a third of them down to ground level. This will encourage new growth to shoot from the base. Old weak plants in particular can be rejuvenated in this way.

Winter Protection Although hardy, hydrangea come into growth early during spring and new shoots can be prone to an attack from late frosts. This is another reason for leaving last year's flower heads on until spring.

Pests & Diseases Generally trouble-free, although honey fungus can kill shrubs quickly.

~

The first of any hydrangea species to bloom, the broad, subtle pink-purple flower heads of Hydrangea aspera *ssp.* sargentiana *can cover this superb woodland shrub when they appear in midsummer.*

Few flowers can match the early summer display of the ice-blue Meconopsis *x* sheldonii.

~

PROPAGATION

Semi-ripe cuttings can be taken from late summer to early autumn. These should be 10-15cm (4-6in) long and should be inserted into a cutting mix. Better rooting occurs if cuttings are placed in a heated propagation case, although some success can be achieved by inserting them into a cold frame. Seeds can be sown during the spring in a coarse seed mix and placed into a cold frame. The seed is very small, so it's important not to sow it too thickly or to cover it completely.

OTHER VARIETIES

H. quercifolia H & S: 1.5 x 2.75m (5 x 9ft). An interesting species from the United States, it forms a low spreading shrub with dark green, deeply cut leaves which are very downy. The flowers are white and produced in dense clusters during summer. *H. petiolaris* H & S: 6 x 3m 20 x 10ft). An attractive, deciduous, self-clinging climber, its foliage is dark olive green and beautifully set off against its cinnamon-red stems. The flowers are white and numerous. It is a very useful plant for covering a cold wall.

Meconopsis x *sheldonii*

(M. GRANDIS X M. BETONICIFOLIA)

A striking robust hybrid which can reach a height of 1.25-1.5m (4-5ft) and a spread of 60cm (2ft), *M.* x *sheldonii* makes an excellent garden plant. Its parents originate in the Himalayas, but this hybrid was raised at Oxted, in Surrey, in 1937. It forms very leafy clumps with neatly toothed leaves. The beautiful, deep blue flowers are produced in large quantities during early summer and are 3cm (1½in) across. It is not overly hardy, but will tolerate a temperature of -7°C (20°F).

Requiring cool, moist, woodland conditions, it looks wonderful when set off against a backdrop of white azalea or when planted with white foxgloves (*Digitalis purpurea* 'Alba'), or it can be planted in solitary drifts where it will make a dramatic planting in any garden.

CULTIVATION

Site Selection Meconopsis require a cool, moist position in dappled or part-shade. Strong sunlight will fade flowers quickly and intense hot sunlight will burn the foliage. Plant them in amongst shrubs or within the shade of a tree – not one that is shallow rooting, i.e. a beech or hornbeam, otherwise the soil will dry out during summer. Alternatively plant within the shade of a north- or east-facing wall, as long as the soil is sufficiently deep. I have seen meconopsis planted successfully up against hedges in deep soil, the hedge providing the shade and shelter from strong winds.

Soil These plants need a deep, moisture-retentive but free-draining soil which is fertile and full of organic matter. Meconopsis will not tolerate soils that dry out during summer or wet, heavy soils with drainage problems. Both clay and sandy soils will have to be improved with plenty of organic matter.

Alkaline soils will also benefit from the addition of plenty of organic matter to raise their acidity, but plants are difficult to establish and sulk on excessively alkaline soils. In such a case I would change the soil in the planting position and replace it with a neutral to acidic, free-draining loam with added organic matter.

Planting Prepare the soil thoroughly with lots of additional organic matter. I favour leaf mould and bark chippings, but garden compost will also do. I know a nurseryman who swears that the best thing is well-rotted farmyard manure. I thought this to be too strong, but his meconopsis were some of the best I have ever seen. Plants are normally planted out during spring.

Potted plants bought during the summer months should be planted as soon as possible so that they can quickly settle into a cooler moister environment rather than being in a pot. It is vital that they are planted at the same depth as they were in the pot; plant too deep and they could suffocate.

When planting, avoid too much root disturbance and try not to get any soil on the leaves as it is difficult to remove. Also take care not to bend the foliage too much: the leaf stalks are brittle and snap easily. Water in well after planting and mulch with leaf mould.

AFTERCARE

Feeding Providing the soil has been properly prepared meconopsis will require no additional feeding. Plants grown in pots may require a fortnightly feed with a liquid manure or equivalent through the growing season.

Pruning The only pruning required is the removal of dead foliage at the end of the year. But if you prune any flower spikes that develop on plants in the first year of planting in the garden, it will make them put all their energy into the production of new rosettes of leaves, providing better, stronger plants that are more likely to flower for many years to come.

Winter Protection Plants don't like cold, wet winters with temperatures well below freezing for months at a time. In mild, wet regions a simple cloche made up of wire and small panes of glass will keep rain off the foliage and prevent the plants from rotting.

Pests & Diseases Plants are generally untroubled by pests, apart from the occasional aphid attack on developing flower buds, but fungal attacks can be a problem.

During summer the undersurfaces of the leaves, together with the flower stalks and seed capsules can become infected with a downy mildew which shows up as furry grey patches. It is rarely fatal, apart from when it infects seedlings. It should be treated with a fungicide.

PROPAGATION

Plants of *M.* x *sheldonii* should be lifted and divided at least once every three to five years and replanted to maintain vigour. This is usually done during the spring or autumn, or immediately after flowering, providing the plants are watered well until they are re-established.

Plants can also be raised from seed. As *M. x sheldonii* is a hybrid it has to be maintained by vegetative propagation, but many other meconopsis are monocarpic. These must be raised from seed, generally produced freely on flowered plants.

Seed is best sown when it is ripe – usually late summer when it will germinate – and should be kept 13-18°C (55-65°F). It should be sown in equal parts peat and sand. Do not cover the seeds with compost and make sure they are in a partly lit position.

When the seedlings are large enough to handle, prick them out into individual 7-cm (3-in) pots so they can the be grown on before being planted out either in a nursery bed or their final flowering position the following autumn.

OTHER VARIETIES

M. betonicifolia H & S: 150 x 60cm (5 x 2ft). Easy to grow, the length of life of this popular plant can be increased if the developing flower spikes are cut off in its first two years. After this, sufficient rosettes should have been produced to ensure a reliable and plentiful crop of flowers for future years. Its flower colour varies, particularly from seed-grown plants, between mauve and pink and sky blue. *M. regia* H & S: 150 x 60cm (5 x 2ft). This large monocarpic species from Nepal is well worth growing for its winter foliage. Each leaf is covered in dense golden hairs so tightly packed together that they hold water droplets like beads. Its flower spike is covered in large, deep yellow flowers 6cm (2in) in diameter.

MORE WOODLAND PLANTS TO TRY

~

Arisaema consanguineum H & S: 100 x 40cm (36 x 16in). This dramatic herbaceous perennial has mottled, dark green stems and leaves which radiate out at the top. In early summer it produces a flower spike with an outer spathe that is greeny-brown with white stripes. The inner spadix is green. It can produce vivid scarlet fruits in autumn if pollinated. Hardy down to -10°C (14°F) or -15°C (5°F), it likes a humus-rich, well-drained soil

Eucryphia x nymansensis 'Nymansay' H & S: 5 x 3m (15 x 10ft). A handsome evergreen shrub whose branches are covered in numerous, white, saucer-shaped flowers in late summer. Hardy down to -10°C (14°F) or -15°C (5°F), if it is given shelter from cold winds, it

prefers a woodland environment with its roots shaded to keep them cool.

Fatsia japonica H & S: 4 x 3m (12 x 10ft). An evergreen shrub with large, glossy, lobed leaves, it produces small, creamy-white flowers which appear in autumn. These are sometimes followed by shining black berries. Hardy to -10°C (14°F), but preferring warmer temperatures, it thrives in a humus-rich soil in shade.

Pileostegia viburnoïdes H & S: 5 x 4m (15 x 12ft). This has long leathery leaves and its flowers are small and creamy-white and appear in terminal clusters from late summer to early autumn. It is hardy down to -10 C (14°F)

and likes a moist, humus-rich soil in dappled or full shade.

Pseudowintera colorata H & S: 1 x 1.25m (3 x 4ft). A delightful evergreen shrub with unusual mottled grey-white foliage that is edged purple-red. Its flowers appear in summer in clusters and are small and greenish-yellow. It is hardy down to -10°C (14°F) and it likes a moist, humus-rich soil in the shade.

Schizophragma integrifolium H & S: 10 x 7m (30 x 21ft). An elegant, deciduous, slow-growing climber which has oval, dark green leaves and produces large white bracts of flowers in summer. Usually planted to grow up established trees, it likes a moist, humus-rich soil and is hardy down to -15°C (5°F).

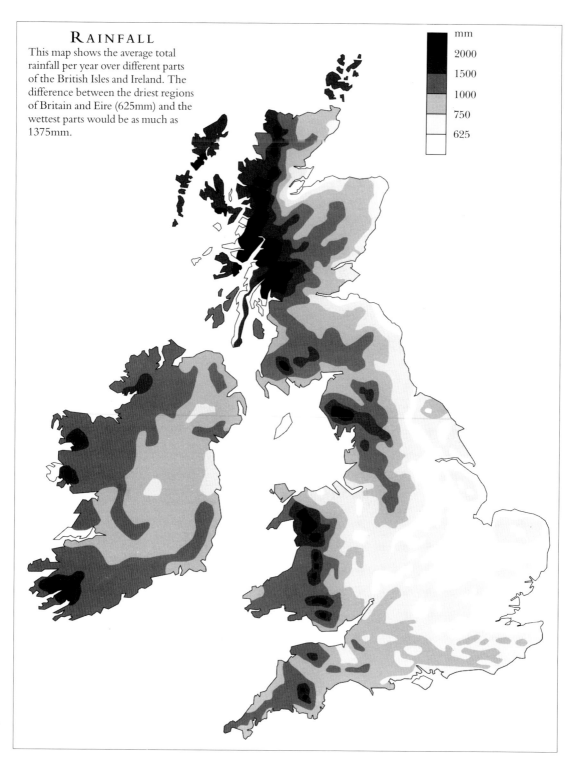

RAINFALL

This map shows the average total rainfall per year over different parts of the British Isles and Ireland. The difference between the driest regions of Britain and Eire (625mm) and the wettest parts would be as much as 1375mm.

mm
2000
1500
1000
750
625

FROSTS

It is very difficult to give an accurate time for the length of the growing season throughout the British Isles and Ireland. These two maps indicate the average dates of the last and first frosts in different areas and can be used as a rough guide to the length of the growing season in each part of these countries.

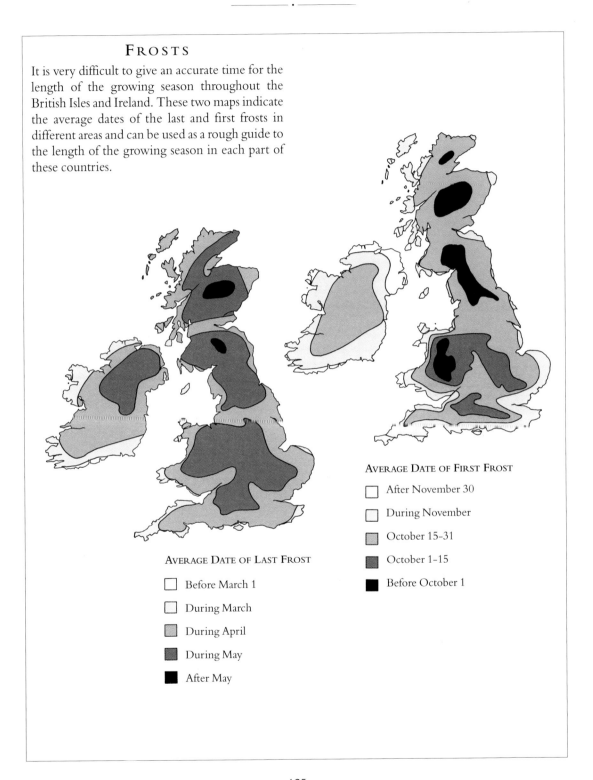

AVERAGE DATE OF FIRST FROST

▢ After November 30

▢ During November

▨ October 15–31

▨ October 1–15

■ Before October 1

AVERAGE DATE OF LAST FROST

▢ Before March 1

▢ During March

▨ During April

▨ During May

■ After May

Useful Addresses

You will find most of the plants featured in this book available at any one of the plant centres or nurseries listed

Abbotsbury Sub Tropical Gardens
Abbotsbury
Nr Weymouth
Dorset DT3 4LA
Tel: 01305 871

The Bluebell Nursery
Blackfordby
Swadlincote
Derbyshire DE11 8AJ
Tel: 01283 22091

Bodnant Garden Nursery Ltd
Tal-y-Cafn
Colwyn Bay
Clwyd LL28 5RE
Tel: 01492 650460

The Botanic Nursery
Rookery Nurseries
Cottles Lane
Atworth
Nr Melksham
Wiltshire SN12 8NU
Tel: 01225 706597/706631

Cannington College Plant Centre
Cannington
Bridgewater
Somerset TA5 2LS
Tel: 01278 286231

Beth Chatto Gardens Ltd
Elmstead Market
Colchester
Essex CO7 7DB
Tel: 01206 825933

Craigieburn Castle Plants
Craigieburn House
Moffat
Dumfriesshire DG10 9LF
Tel: 01683 21250

Hardy Exotics
Gilly Lane
Whitecross
Penzance
Cornwall TR20 8BZ
Tel: 01736 740660

Hippopottering Nursery
Orchard House
Brackenhill Road
Haxey
Nr Doncaster
South Yorkshire DN9 2LR
Tel: 01427 752185

Jungle Giants
Plough Farm
Wigmore
Herefordshire HR6 9UW
Tel: 01568 86708

Kinlochaich House
Garden Plants Centre
Appin
Argyll PA38 4BD
Tel: 0163173 342

The Palm Centre
563 Upper Richmond Road West
London SW14 7ED
Tel: 0181 876223

Plant World
St Marychurch Road
Newton Abbot
South Devon
Tel: 01803 872939

Seaside Nursery
Claddaghduff
Co. Galway
Eire
Tel: 09544 687

Special Plants
Laurels Farm
Upper Wraxall
Chippenham
Wiltshire SN14 7AG
Tel: 01225 891686

Trewidden Estate Nursery
Trewidden Gardens
Penzance
Cornwall TR20 8TT
Tel: 01736 62087

J. Vanderplank
Lampley Road
Kingston Seymour
Clevedon
Avon BS21 6XS
Tel: 01934 833350

Waterwheel Nursery
Bully Hole Bottom
Usk Road
Shirenewton
Chepstow
Gwent NP6 6SA
Tel: 01291 641577